The Molly Goldberg Jewish Cookbook

The Molly Goldberg Jewish Cookbook

By Gertrude Berg and Myra Waldo

Drawings by Susanne Suba

Book-of-the-Month Club
New York

INTRODUCTION

This is My Cookbook. So how did I come to write a cookbook? I had to protect myself, that's how. To make a long story, I had to. Necessity is the mother of invention, no? So I'm a mother, no? So I wrote a cookbook. And what was the big necessity that I should put recipes in a book? When I cook for my family I don't have trouble. But when someone, Mrs. Herman, for an instance, asks me, "How do you make this or how do you make that?" do I know? Of course I know, but can I tell her? Of course I can, but it's easier to show her. So I have to say to her, "Come into my kitchen and I'll make you up." That takes time, not that I begrudge such a dear friend my time, certainly not, but I mean if I'm going to show Mrs. Herman and all my neighbors how I cook something, who's going to make supper? My Jake would complain.

So My Rosie had an idea. "Ma," she said, "I'll stand on your shoulder while you cook and I'll write you down." Only in better English she said it. And that's what happened. I cooked and she wrote. For an instance, when I make my pudding I let it bake for a jitney. How long is a jitney? Rosie timed me, and jitney is never twice the same. It's from when it begins to boil until it's finished baking. And if I say,

5

Introduction

"Throw an eye every however," My Rosie says that means "stir occasionally." I didn't know that.

But as everyone knows, there can be many a slip betwixt the cup and the lip. Even with Rosie standing on my shoulder mistakes can happen. So what would be if the recipe had a teaspoon too much or an egg didn't get counted? You wouldn't have a perfect whatever. Not that My Rosie isn't smart, but My Jake comes in to taste and Sammy comes in for a remark and David remembers a recipe and before you know it you can lose your place.

That would be all right if you lived next door and could yoo-hoo me a question, but if you bought this book already you don't live within my distance, so you see everything must be correct—to a T. So the next voice you read will be a lady who knows whereof, Myra Waldo. And what you read will be correct and very scientific. A doctor she's not, but a cook, yes indeed, and I know whereof I speak.

So everything in this book is very scientific right down to the last snick-snack. I didn't know science could be so tasty, but like Jake says, "You have to translate your words into standard terms." So here it is, and it didn't lose a thing in the translation. . . . I can assure you.

Very truly yours,
Molly Goldberg

P.S. Read further and you'll meet my friend Myra Waldo.

Watching Molly cook was a wonderful experience. I think the secret of her success is that she likes to cook, and delights in having her family and friends praise her food. She is warmhearted and enjoys extending hospitality, and to her, hospitality means smiling faces around the table eating the food that she has prepared.

Molly cooks effortlessly and the results are always good. Of course she had always measured her ingredients by the pinch, the sprinkle, and the handful. But not everyone's pinch, sprinkle, and handful are the same. She made a spongecake, for example, by adding just the amount of flour that was necessary, but only Molly knew when the proper amount had been added. But this would never do for a cookbook. I was at her side (although I did not stand on her shoulder as Rosie did) and carefully measured each ingredient as it was added and timed each cooking period.

She cooked many dishes of all sorts for me, and I had a wonderful time tasting her many talented creations. The best of them are in this book and we hope that you will like them.

A brief explanation is in order about Jewish cookery. (A discussion of kosher food appears in a separate chapter.) Not all Jewish people come from one country, and the countries of origin have left their imprints upon the cooking. Examples of dishes which they have adopted would include such things as paprikas and breaded meats from Austria; dumplings, cabbage and sauerkraut dishes, poppy seed desserts from Czechoslovakia; sweet and sour preparations, potato pancakes, *gefilte* fish, fruit soups from Germany; herring dishes, thick soups from Holland; goulash and *strudel* from Hungary; pickled fish, *pierogen*, mushroom dishes from Poland; corn-meal mixtures, meat and vegetable stews from Rumania; *borscht*, *blintzes*, *kasha* from Russia; and eggplant preparations from the Near and Middle East.

It will be noticed that the type of shortening has not been specified. This is because people who are kosher do not mix meat and dairy products. You are at liberty to use butter or any other shortening to which you are accustomed.

All of the recipes in the book are usable and readily prepared. The food is well flavored although not necessarily highly seasoned. Many of the dishes may be prepared the day before they are to be served, which will assist the busy housewife. There are also many dishes which are really a meal in themselves. All the ingredients called for are easily obtainable. All recipes serve six.

Molly and I enjoyed working together. Our hope is that reading this book and cooking the recipes will bring to you some of the warmth and hospitality of Molly's kitchen.

Myra Waldo

CONTENTS

Contents

ALL RECIPES SERVE SIX

Appetizers

Appetizers. What does that mean? To me it means something to tickle the appetite, a coming attraction for the meal no matter what. An appetizer should be chosen to go with the meal, not just willy-nilly. For an instance, My Uncle David loves Chopped Chicken Livers. He eats it for an appetizer and then he takes a plate of it for the main dish, and if there was a Chopped Chicken Liver dessert he would have that too. I'm not saying that Chopped Liver is the answer to all your appetizing problems, far from it. I'm only saying start your meal with an appetizer.

EGGPLANT APPETIZER

1 medium eggplant
2 onions
3 tomatoes
2 slices white bread, trimmed
¼ cup vinegar
2 teaspoons salt
½ teaspoon freshly ground black
    pepper
1 teaspoon sugar
3 tablespoons salad oil

Place the eggplant on a baking sheet. Bake in a 375° oven for 45 minutes, or until tender. Cool and peel.

Chop the onions very fine. Add the tomatoes and eggplant. Chop fine. Soak the bread in the vinegar, and add, together with the salt, pepper, sugar, and oil. Chop until very smooth and well blended. Correct seasoning; the mixture should be fairly spicy.

Serve cold as an appetizer or relish.

IKRA

CAVIAR APPETIZER

1 pound pike roe
1 tablespoon salt
½ cup olive oil
2 tablespoons lemon juice
1 tablespoon ice water
1 onion, chopped fine
10 ripe olives, sliced thin

Wash the roe carefully and remove the veins. Place in a bowl and sprinkle with salt. Chill for at least 6 hours. Rinse and drain.

Beat the roe with a fork for 1 minute. Gradually add the olive oil, drop by drop, beating constantly. Add the lemon juice and ice water. Beat all together until the mixture is firm and each egg is separate. Sprinkle the onion and olives over the roe. Chill.

Serve cold with quarters of lemon. Thin slices of dark bread are the usual accompaniment.

KNOBL FISH

SPICY FISH

5 cloves garlic, minced
2 teaspoons salt
½ teaspoon freshly ground black pepper
1 tablespoon paprika
6 slices fish (carp or whitefish)
2 tablespoons shortening

Mix the garlic, salt, pepper, and paprika to a smooth paste. Rub it into the fish very well. Set aside for 2 hours.

Melt the shortening in a baking dish. Place the fish in it. Bake in a 275° oven for 2 hours, or until the fish is very dry and browned. Turn the fish frequently while baking. Remove from oven and let cool.

Serve cold.

CHOPPED CHICKEN LIVERS

½ cup shortening
2 onions, sliced
1 pound chicken livers, washed
and drained
2 hard-cooked egg yolks
1½ teaspoons salt
¼ teaspoon freshly ground black
pepper

Melt ¼ cup of the shortening in a skillet. Add the onions. Sauté for 10 minutes, stirring frequently. Remove the onions and set aside. Melt the remaining ¼ cup of shortening in the same skillet. Sauté the livers in it for 10 minutes, stirring occasionally. Grind the onions, livers, and egg yolks in a food chopper, or chop very fine in a wooden bowl. Add the salt and pepper and mix well together. Chill.

Serve as an *hors d'oeuvre*, or as an appetizer on a bed of lettuce leaves. It is often customary to pour a teaspoon of rendered chicken fat over each portion.

BAKED HERRING

6 fillets of salt herring
4 onions, sliced
½ cup flour
4 tablespoons butter
3 tablespoons heavy cream

Soak the herring in cold water to cover overnight. Change the water at least twice. Drain. Rinse, and drain again.

Place the onions in a saucepan with water to cover. Bring to a boil and cook for 2 minutes. Drain. Dip the herring in the flour, coating both sides lightly. Arrange the herring in a buttered baking dish. Spread the onions over them. Dot with the butter.

Bake in a 400° oven for 20 minutes. Add the cream and bake for 10 minutes longer.

If you think Shakespeare is a friend of mine you're right. Of course I have never had the pleasure, but still I feel like he's an old friend. Why? Because he said some wise things, like for instance, "a rose by any other name . . ." Now that's smart, but of course he wasn't talking about herring. For me herring is wonderful any way you make it, chopped or pickled or by any other name it's unmistakable, but my own favorite is fried. I am sure that you will agree with my decision.

FRIED HERRING
À LA WILLIAM SHAKESPEARE

> 6 fillets of salt herring
> ½ cup flour
> ¼ cup bread crumbs
> 2 eggs, beaten
> ½ cup shortening

Soak the herring in cold water to cover overnight. Change the water at least twice. Drain well and rinse again. If a very mild herring is desired, use milk instead of water.

Mix the flour and bread crumbs together. Dip the herring in the flour mixture, then in the beaten eggs, and again in the flour mixture, coating both sides well.

Melt half of the shortening in a skillet. Fry the herring until browned on both sides, about 5 minutes on each side. Add more shortening as needed.

Serve with fried onions and boiled potatoes if desired.

HERRING SALAD

> 3 fillets of salt herring, sliced
>   into ½-inch pieces
> 1 onion, sliced thin
> 2 green peppers, diced
> 1 cup shredded cabbage
> 2 tomatoes, cubed
> 1 cup shredded lettuce
> 6 radishes, sliced thin
> 3 tablespoons olive oil or salad
>   oil
> ⅓ cup vinegar
> ¼ teaspoon freshly ground black
>   pepper
> 2 teaspoons sugar

In a glass or wooden bowl, combine the herring, onion, green peppers, cabbage, tomatoes, lettuce, and radishes. Toss lightly.

Mix together the oil, vinegar, pepper, and sugar. Pour over the herring mixture. Chill for 1 hour.

PICKLED HERRING

> 6 salt herring fillets
> 1 cup vinegar
> ¼ cup water
> 2 teaspoons sugar
> 3 onions, sliced thin
> 1½ teaspoons pickling spice
> 2 bay leaves
> ½ cup sour cream (optional)

Soak the herring in water to cover overnight. Change the water twice. If desired, the herring fillets may be cut into slices.

Combine the vinegar, water, and sugar in a saucepan. Bring to a boil, and boil for 2 minutes.

Arrange layers of herring, onions, pickling spice, and bay leaves in a glass jar or bowl. Mix the sour cream (if desired) with the vinegar mixture, and pour over the herring. Cover, and allow to marinate for 48 hours in the refrigerator before serving.

HERRING APPETIZER

4 salt herring fillets
3 tomatoes, chopped
¾ cup water
2 teaspoons sugar
2 teaspoons chopped dill
2 teaspoons chopped parsley
2 scallions (green onions), sliced
½ cup chopped ripe olives
2 tablespoons vinegar
4 tablespoons olive oil

Soak the herring in water to cover overnight. Drain. Rinse again and cut into ½-inch slices.

Combine the tomatoes, water, and sugar in a saucepan. Cook over low heat for 15 minutes. Mix well. Add the dill, parsley, scallions, olives, vinegar, and oil. Cook for 5 minutes. Pour over the herring. Chill.

Serve very cold on lettuce leaves.

BAKED HERRING APPETIZER

5 herring fillets
3 tablespoons butter
2 onions, chopped
6 slices white bread, trimmed
1 apple, peeled
1 cup sour cream
3 tablespoons bread crumbs

Soak the herring in water to cover overnight. Drain.

Melt the butter in a skillet. Add the onions. Sauté for 10 minutes, stirring frequently.

Chop the herring, bread, apple, and sautéed onions together. Add the sour cream. Mix well. Pour into a buttered baking dish. Sprinkle with the bread crumbs.

Bake in a 400° oven for 30 minutes.

CHOPPED HERRING

3 salt herring
½ onion
1 apple, peeled and cored
4 hard-cooked egg yolks
2 slices white bread, trimmed
¼ cup cider vinegar
3 tablespoons salad oil
1 teaspoon sugar

Soak the herring in water to cover overnight, changing the water at least twice. Drain well. Fillet the herring carefully.

Chop the onion and apple together. Add the herring and egg yolks. Chop again. Soak the bread in the vinegar, and add, together with the oil and sugar. Chop until very fine and well blended.

Serve cold as an appetizer, cocktail spread, or on lettuce leaves as a fish course.

19

When I asked all my friends what they would like to be remembered for in my cookbook each one gave me their favorite recipe. From Mrs. Herman I didn't had to ask. I already knew. When I go to her house for a little tea we always have Scrambled Eggs and Salmon, and when the girls go out all together and we stop for a bite, Mrs. Herman has Scrambled Eggs and Salmon, and when she comes by me for whatever and I have it in the house, what do you think we have? Here's Mrs. Herman's favorite. It's her recipe that she got from her mother. I think it runs in the family.

SCRAMBLED EGGS AND SALMON À LA MRS. HERMAN

4 tablespoons shortening
3 onions, chopped
2 green peppers, diced
¼ pound smoked salmon, coarsely shredded
6 eggs
3 tablespoons cold water
¼ teaspoon freshly ground black pepper

Melt half the shortening in a skillet. Add the onions and green peppers. Sauté for 15 minutes, stirring frequently. Add the salmon, and sauté for 5 minutes. Add the remaining shortening.

Beat the eggs, water, and pepper together. Pour over the salmon mixture. Cook over low heat, stirring constantly until the mixture is set, but do not overcook.

CHOPPED EGGS AND ONIONS

2 onions
8 hard-cooked eggs
1½ teaspoons salt
¼ teaspoon freshly ground black
  pepper
4 tablespoons rendered chicken
  fat
Lettuce leaves

Chop the onions very fine. Add the eggs, and continue chopping. Add the salt, pepper, and chicken fat. Mix lightly. Correct seasoning. Serve on lettuce leaves.

MARINATED FRIED FISH

2 teaspoons salt
½ cup flour
2 eggs, beaten
2 tablespoons cold water
6 fillets of sole, or similar fish
4 tablespoons shortening
1 cup cider vinegar
¼ cup boiling water
2 tablespoons sugar
2 onions, sliced thin
2 cloves garlic, minced
½ teaspoon pickling spice

Mix the salt and flour together. Beat the eggs and cold water together. Dip the fish in the flour mixture and then in the egg and water.

Heat the shortening in a skillet, and fry the fish in it until browned on both sides. Place the fish in a bowl or glass container.

Combine the vinegar, boiling water, sugar, onions, garlic, and pickling spice in a saucepan. Boil for 2 minutes. Pour over the fish. Cover, and marinate in refrigerator for at least 4 hours before serving. Serve cold.

CHOPPED BRAINS

2 calves' brains
1 tablespoon vinegar
2 teaspoons salt
2 onions, chopped
4 tablespoons olive oil
¼ teaspoon freshly ground black pepper
3 tablespoons lemon juice

Wash the brains. Place in a saucepan with water to cover. Add the vinegar and salt. Bring to a boil. Cover and cook over low heat for 30 minutes. Drain well. Remove the membrane. Chop the brains. Add the onions, olive oil, pepper, and lemon juice. Mix well. Chill.

VEGETABLE CHICKEN LIVERS

2 pounds string beans
2 cups water
2 teaspoons salt
3 tablespoons salad oil
1 onion, chopped
2 hard-cooked egg yolks
¼ teaspoon freshly ground black pepper

Combine the string beans and water in a saucepan. Bring to a boil and add 1 teaspoon of the salt. Cook over medium heat for 20

22

minutes, or until very tender. Drain. Grind the beans in a food chopper, or chop very fine.

Heat the oil in a skillet. Sauté the onion in it for 10 minutes, stirring frequently. Add to the beans, together with the egg yolks. Chop until very fine and well blended. Add the pepper and remaining salt. Mix well. Pack into a bowl. Chill.

Serve on lettuce leaves.

For such a little thing to have four names is a little beyond me, but it only goes to prove that when something is good, it's good in any language. For instance, I always called it nahit, my grocer calls it chick-peas. Mrs. Maggi upstairs calls it cecci and Mrs. Flores from the Parents and Teachers calls it garbanzos. So there you are. Four names for one little bean and the translation of each is—delicious.

NAHIT

CHICK-PEAS

1 pound chick-peas
2 teaspoons salt
½ teaspoon freshly ground black pepper

Wash the chick-peas. Cover with water and soak overnight. Drain. Add fresh water to cover. Bring to a boil. Cover, and cook over low heat for 1½ hours, or until tender. Drain. Sprinkle with the salt and pepper. Cook over low heat for 3 minutes, shaking the pan constantly. Let cool, but do not chill.

Serve as a cocktail appetizer or as a snack.

BAKED TONGUE ROLLS

2 cups chopped cooked tongue
½ cup finely chopped dill pickles
6 tablespoons melted shortening
6 hard rolls (oblong or round)

Mix the tongue, pickles, and 2 tablespoons of the shortening together. Preheat oven to 375°.

Cut a 1-inch piece from one side of the rolls and scoop out carefully. Stuff with the tongue mixture. Brush the rolls with the remaining shortening. Place on a baking pan.

Bake for 15 minutes, or until lightly browned.

Serve as a luncheon dish or late snack. Small versions of this dish make excellent *hors d'oeuvres*.

NOTE: If a smoother mixture is desired, grind tongue and pickles together.

GRATED BLACK RADISH

2 black radishes, peeled
1 onion (optional)
¼ cup rendered chicken or goose fat
1½ teaspoons salt
¼ teaspoon freshly ground black pepper

Grate the radishes and onion on a medium grater. Add the chicken fat, salt, and pepper. Toss lightly. Chill.

Serve on lettuce leaves.

Soups

Soup in America is very refined. But when I was a girl, soup was for every day and not just for company or was it the kind of a day for soup? People ate soup because it was the cheapest way to feed the most people on the least food. Nowadays soup is a special dish and it's not such a necessity, but sometimes when the budget is low it's a good thing to remember.

Soup is really a Mr. Jekyll and Mr. Hyde food. For company it's fancy, for every day it's cheap and easy to make, and it's also good if you feel like a plate. In your best dishes it's very distinguished indeed, and in your everyday dishes it's soup, and if your family is like my family it's not a meal without it. Sammy's favorite soup is any kind of soup so long as it has lots of things in it like noodles, mandel, kasha, kreplach, and maybe a few other things too. Sometimes the soup is so thick with different things, there's no room for the soup.

CREAM OF LIMA BEAN SOUP

1½ cups dried lima beans
6 tablespoons butter
6 scallions (green onions) or 2
  onions, chopped
7 cups water
2 teaspoons salt
¼ teaspoon white pepper
1 cup light cream

Wash the beans. Place in a saucepan with water to cover. Bring to a boil, remove from the heat, and let soak for 1 hour. Drain.

Melt the butter in a saucepan. Add the scallions and sauté for 5 minutes, stirring frequently. Add the beans and the 7 cups of water. Cover and cook over low heat for 2 hours, or until beans are soft. Force through a sieve or purée in an electric blender. Return the mixture to a saucepan. Add the salt, pepper, and cream. Heat and serve.

NOODLES AND MILK SOUP

4 tablespoons butter
3 tablespoons flour
6 cups milk
1½ teaspoons salt
1 tablespoon sugar
¼ pound fine noodles, half
cooked, drained

Melt the butter in a saucepan. Add the flour, stirring until smooth. Add the milk gradually, stirring constantly until the boiling point. Add the salt, sugar, and noodles.
Cook over low heat for 5 minutes. Serve hot.

LENTIL SOUP

1 tablespoon shortening
1 onion, chopped
1½ cups lentils, washed and
drained
2 carrots, scraped and sliced
7 cups water
1 tablespoon salt
¼ teaspoon pepper
6 frankfurters, sliced

Melt the shortening in a skillet. Sauté the onion in it for 5 minutes. Add the lentils, carrots, and water. Bring to a boil; add the salt and pepper; cover and cook over low heat for 3 hours. Force through a sieve or purée in an electric blender. Add the frankfurters and cook 10 minutes longer.

TOMATO SOUP

6 tomatoes, chopped, or 1 can
(⚹2) tomatoes
½ cup water
1 onion, chopped
1½ teaspoons salt
1 tablespoon lemon juice
1 tablespoon sugar
½ cup milk, scalded
½ cup light cream, scalded

Combine the tomatoes, water, onion, and salt in a saucepan. Cook over low heat for 30 minutes. Add the lemon juice and sugar. Cook 5 minutes. Correct seasoning. The soup should be tart and slightly sweet. Force through a sieve or purée in an electric blender. Add the milk and cream, mixing steadily. Reheat and serve.

PICKLE SOUP

5 dried mushrooms
7 cups water
2 onions, chopped
1 clove garlic, minced
1 carrot, sliced
1 bay leaf
3 potatoes, peeled and diced
1½ teaspoons salt
⅛ teaspoon freshly ground black
   pepper
2 kosher-style pickles, diced
2 tablespoons chopped parsley

Soak the mushrooms in water to cover for 1 hour. Drain well.
   Place them in a saucepan with the 7 cups of water, onions, garlic, carrot, and bay leaf. Bring to a boil. Cover and cook over low heat

for 1 hour. Discard the bay leaf. Force the mixture through a sieve. Add the potatoes, salt, pepper, and pickles. Cook over low heat for 15 minutes, adding a little water if soup is too thick. Correct seasoning. Add parsley and serve.

> *This is nobodies' recipe. It was handed down. Borscht is more than a soup, it's a weather vane. When my family says they want hot borscht I know winter is coming, and when they want cold borscht I know how far can spring be behind? When I make cold borscht I am always in the middle of putting the clothes in the camphor and when I make hot borscht it's time already to get the winter clothes out of the closet. So borscht is not only a soup, it's a friend that comes and goes with the robins.*

COLD BORSCHT

COLD BEET SOUP

8 beets, washed and peeled
1 onion, chopped fine
2½ quarts water
1 tablespoon salt
⅓ cup lemon juice
3 tablespoons sugar
2 eggs
1 cup sour cream

Combine the beets, onion, water, and salt in a saucepan. Bring to a boil and cook over medium heat for 1 hour. Add the lemon juice and sugar and cook for 30 minutes. Correct seasoning; the soup may require a little more sugar or lemon juice, depending upon the sweetness of the beets.

Beat the eggs in a bowl. Gradually add 3 cups of the soup, beating constantly to prevent curdling. Return this mixture to the balance of the soup, beating steadily. Remove all of the beets from the soup. Grate 5 of the beets and return them to the soup. The remaining beets may be used in a cold salad. Chill the soup, and serve very cold with a spoonful of sour cream in each plate.

NOTE: If a very thick soup is desired, place the remaining beets in an electric blender with 2 cups of the soup, and run the machine until the mixture is smooth. Add the mixture to the soup.

HOT MEAT BORSCHT

HOT BEET SOUP

8 large beets, peeled
2 onions, chopped
2 cloves garlic, minced
3 quarts water
2 pounds short ribs or breast flank
Beef bones
2½ teaspoons salt
½ teaspoon freshly ground black pepper
1 cup coarsely shredded cabbage
⅓ cup lemon juice
4 tablespoons sugar
2 eggs, beaten

Grate half of the beets. Combine the grated beets with the whole beets, onions, garlic, water, meat, and bones in a large saucepan. Bring to a boil; skim off the top. Cover, and cook over medium heat for 1½ hours. Add the salt, pepper, and cabbage, and stir. Cook uncovered for 45 minutes. Add the lemon juice and sugar. Cook for 15 minutes. Correct seasoning. The soup should have both a sweet and sour taste, so add more lemon juice or sugar if necessary. Remove the whole beets and the bones.

Beat the eggs in a bowl. Gradually add about 3 cups of the soup, beating steadily to prevent curdling. Return this mixture to the balance of the soup, mixing steadily. Reheat, but do not allow to boil.

Serve the soup with the meat on the side in a separate dish. When served with boiled potatoes, this constitutes a complete meal in one dish.

VEGETABLE SOUP

4 tablespoons shortening
2 onions, sliced
2 carrots, sliced
1 cup shredded cabbage
2 stalks celery
½ pound green peas, shelled
¼ pound string beans, halved
¼ pound lima beans, shelled
7 cups water
2 teaspoons salt
¼ teaspoon freshly ground black pepper
½ teaspoon sugar
2 tomatoes, peeled and chopped
2 potatoes, peeled and diced
¼ pound fine noodles, cooked and drained
1 tablespoon chopped parsley

Melt the shortening in a saucepan. Add the onions and sauté for 10 minutes, stirring frequently. Add the carrots, cabbage, celery, green peas, string beans, and lima beans. Cover and cook over low heat for 10 minutes. Add the water, salt, pepper, sugar, tomatoes, and potatoes. Cover, and cook over medium heat for 30 minutes. Add noodles and parsley. Cook for 5 minutes additional.

BARLEY AND BEAN SOUP

> 1 cup lima beans
> 4 tablespoons pearl barley
> 8 cups water
> 2 onions, chopped
> 1 carrot, grated
> 2 teaspoons salt
> ½ teaspoon freshly ground black pepper
> 3 tablespoons butter
> 1 cup light cream

Wash the beans thoroughly. Cover with water; bring to a boil and soak for 2 hours. Drain.

Soak the barley in water to cover for 2 hours. Drain.

Combine the beans, barley, the 8 cups of water, onions, and carrot in a saucepan. Cover and cook over low heat for 2½ hours, or until beans are tender. Add the salt, pepper, butter, and cream. Cook for 10 minutes additional. Correct seasoning.

> NOTE: If a very smooth soup is desired, purée the mixture in a food mill or electric blender.

WINE SOUP

> 3½ cups sweet red wine
> 1½ cups water
> 3 tablespoons lemon juice
> 4 eggs
> 5 tablespoons sugar
> 1 teaspoon salt

Combine the wine, water, and lemon juice in a saucepan. Bring to a boil, and cook over low heat for 10 minutes.

33

Beat 2 of the eggs and 2 egg yolks (reserving the 2 egg whites). Add 3 tablespoons of the sugar and the salt. Gradually add the wine mixture, stirring constantly to prevent curdling. Chill.

Before serving, beat the egg whites until they begin to stiffen. Add the sugar gradually, beating constantly until stiff.

Serve the soup with a heaping tablespoon of the egg-white meringue on top.

SPLIT PEA SOUP

> 2 cups split peas
> 2½ quarts water
> 1 pound beef (plate flank, breast flank, or chuck)
> Beef bones
> 2 onions, chopped
> 1 carrot, grated
> 1 stalk celery
> 3 sprigs parsley
> 2 potatoes, peeled and sliced
> 2½ teaspoons salt
> ½ teaspoon freshly ground black pepper

Soak the peas in water to cover overnight if presoaked variety is not used. Drain.

Combine the peas, water, beef, beef bones, onions, carrot, celery, and parsley in a saucepan. Cover and cook over low heat for 1½ hours. Add the potatoes, salt, and pepper. Cook for 45 minutes additional, or until the peas are very soft. Remove the meat. Force the soup through a food mill or purée it in an electric blender. Correct seasoning. If too thick, add a little water.

The meat should be cut into small pieces and served in the soup.

My mother-in-law, Jake's mother, taught me a trick. To her it was more than a trick, it was confidence. When she made cabbage soup it lasted her three days. How? The first day it was a meal by itself, with the meat. The second day she served it with the smaller pieces of meat cut up in it, and on the third day it was just soup. When she told me her trick I was flattered, but how could I tell her that's what my mother did also?

CABBAGE SOUP

3 pounds beef (plate flank, breast flank, or brisket)
Beef bones
2½ quarts water
1 can (※2½) tomatoes
2 onions, chopped
4 pounds cabbage, coarsely shredded
2 teaspoons salt
½ teaspoon freshly ground black pepper
½ cup lemon juice
4 tablespoons sugar
½ pound sauerkraut, drained (optional)
2 slices rye bread, trimmed

Combine the beef, beef bones, water, tomatoes, and onions in a saucepan. Bring to a boil. Skim the top. Cover and cook over medium heat for 1 hour. Add the cabbage, salt, and pepper. Cook over low heat for 1 hour. Add the lemon juice, sugar, and sauerkraut. Cook for 15 minutes.

Soak the bread in water for 5 minutes. Drain and add to the soup. Correct seasoning. The soup should have a more sour than sweet taste. Cook for 15 minutes longer, or until the meat is tender.

Serve the soup and meat at the same time. This makes a complete meal in one dish.

DRIED MUSHROOM SOUP

8 dried mushrooms
4 tablespoons fine barley
8 cups water
2 teaspoons salt
½ teaspoon freshly ground black pepper
4 tablespoons shortening
2 onions, chopped fine
2 tablespoons flour
½ cup heavy cream (optional)

Wash the mushrooms thoroughly. Cover with water and soak for 2 hours. Drain and chop.

Combine the mushrooms, barley, water, salt, and pepper in a saucepan. Bring to a boil. Cover and cook over low heat for 1½ hours.

Melt the shortening in a skillet. Add the onions, and sauté for 10 minutes, stirring frequently. Add the flour, stirring until brown. Add to the soup, stirring constantly. Cook over low heat for 30 minutes. Correct seasoning.

Add the cream if desired and serve hot.

FRESH MUSHROOM SOUP

6 tablespoons shortening
2 tablespoons grated onion
¾ pound mushrooms, chopped
1½ teaspoons salt
2 teaspoons chopped parsley
1 teaspoon caraway seeds
(optional)
3 tablespoons flour
3 cups water and 3 cups milk, or
6 cups water

Melt half of the shortening in a skillet. Add the onion, mushrooms, salt, parsley, and caraway seeds. Sauté for 15 minutes, stirring frequently.

Melt the remaining shortening in a saucepan. Add the flour, stirring until smooth. Add the water and milk gradually, stirring constantly until the boiling point. Add the mushroom mixture. Cook over low heat for 10 minutes, stirring frequently. Correct seasoning.

COLD SCHAV

COLD SORREL SOUP

1½ pounds sorrel (sour grass)
6 scallions (green onions), sliced
2½ quarts water
2½ teaspoons salt
4 tablespoons sugar
1 tablespoon lemon juice
2 eggs
½ pint sour cream

Wash the sorrel very thoroughly in several changes of water. Coarsely chop the sorrel, discarding the stems. Combine in a saucepan with the scallions, water, and salt. Bring to a boil. Cover and cook over medium heat for 30 minutes. Add the sugar and lemon juice. Cook for 15 minutes. Correct seasoning. Cook 15 minutes additional.

Beat the eggs in a large bowl. Gradually add the soup to the beaten eggs, stirring constantly to prevent curdling. Chill.

Serve with a tablespoon of sour cream in each portion.

> NOTE: If a very smooth soup is desired, the sorrel may be puréed in a food mill or an electric blender before combining it with the eggs.

CABBAGE AND POTATO SOUP

3 tablespoons shortening
2 onions, chopped
7 cups water
1 pound boneless beef
Beef bones
2 pounds cabbage, shredded
3 potatoes, peeled and diced
2½ teaspoons salt
½ teaspoon freshly ground black pepper
½ teaspoon paprika

Melt the shortening in a saucepan. Add the onions, and sauté for 10 minutes, stirring frequently. Add the water, beef, and beef bones. Bring to a boil. Cover and cook over medium heat for 1¼ hours. Add the cabbage, potatoes, salt, pepper, and paprika. Cook over low heat for 45 minutes. Correct seasoning.

Serve with small pieces of the beef in each plate if desired.

SAUERKRAUT SOUP

1 pound sauerkraut
2 pounds beef
Beef bones
7 cups water
3 tablespoons shortening
2 onions, chopped
½ pound mushrooms, chopped
  (optional)
2 potatoes, peeled and diced
2 teaspoons salt
½ teaspoon freshly ground black
  pepper

Combine the sauerkraut, beef, beef bones, and water in a saucepan. Cover, and cook over medium heat for 1½ hours.

Melt the shortening in a skillet. Add the onions. Sauté for 10 minutes, stirring frequently. Add the mushrooms, and sauté for 5 minutes. Add to the soup, together with the potatoes, salt, and pepper. Cook for ½ hour additional.

Cut the meat into small pieces and serve in the soup.

MEATLESS SAUERKRAUT SOUP

½ pound sauerkraut
½ pound mushrooms, chopped
2 quarts water
2 teaspoons salt
½ teaspoon freshly ground black
  pepper
4 tablespoons shortening
2 onions, chopped
2 tablespoons potato starch or
  cornstarch

Wash the sauerkraut and drain well. Combine it in a saucepan with the mushrooms, water, salt, and pepper. Cover and cook over medium heat for 1 hour.

Heat the shortening in a skillet. Sauté the onions in it for 15 minutes, stirring frequently. Add to the soup. Combine the potato starch with 2 tablespoons of cold water and mix until smooth. Add 1 cup of the hot soup to the potato starch mixture, and mix well. Return the mixture to the balance of the soup, stirring constantly until the boiling point. Cook over low heat for 30 minutes. Correct seasoning.

Serve with a tablespoon of sour cream in each portion if desired.

This soup really comes from Russia, but my friend Mrs. Wiersma says it's Norwegian, and why should I argue? She says she got the recipe from her aunt that lives in Oslo and I got my recipe from my grandmother that lived in Nizhnii Novgorod and that's not in Norway. So what's the distance between the two towns? I'll tell you exactly. Three doors down the hallway. I live in 5C and Mrs. Wiersma lives in 5F, and that's the distance, but Norwegian or Russian or anything else, it's good soup because wherever people live they know a good thing when they see it. I mean taste it.

MRS. WIERSMA'S FRUIT SOUP

3 cups assorted fruit (plums, peaches, pears, cherries, apricots, berries), fresh or dried
5 cups water
2 teaspoons lemon juice
4 tablespoons sugar
2 tablespoons cornstarch
½ cup sour cream

Any combination of fresh or dried fruit may be used. Pit the fruit. Combine the fruit in a saucepan with the water, lemon juice, and sugar. Bring to a boil. Cover and cook over low heat for 20 minutes, or until fruit is very soft. Force through a sieve or purée in an electric blender.

Mix the cornstarch with an equal amount of cold water. Add to the fruit, stirring constantly until the boiling point. Cook over low heat for 5 minutes. Add a little sugar if necessary.

Serve ice cold, with a tablespoon of sour cream in each portion.

MIXED FRUIT SOUP

> 2 oranges, peeled and sliced
> 2 stalks rhubarb, scraped and cut into pieces
> 4 slices pineapple, cubed
> 1 cup berries
> 6 cups water
> 1 cup sugar
> ½ teaspoon salt
> ½ teaspoon cinnamon
> 2 tablespoons lemon juice
> 1 cup sour cream

Combine in a saucepan the oranges, rhubarb, pineapple, berries, water, sugar, salt, cinnamon, and lemon juice. Bring to a boil and cook over low heat for 20 minutes. Chill.

Add the sour cream and serve.

NOTE: If a very smooth soup is desired, purée the mixture in an electric blender or force through a sieve.

COLD CUCUMBER SOUP

> 1 quart buttermilk
> 1 pint sour cream
> 2 cooked or canned beets,
>   chopped
> 2 cucumbers, peeled and diced
> 2 scallions (green onions), sliced
> 1½ teaspoons salt
> 1 tablespoon chopped dill

Mix the buttermilk and sour cream together until smooth. Add the beets, cucumbers, scallions, salt, and dill. Mix well. Chill for at least 2 hours.

Serve with hot, small boiled potatoes.

BARLEY SOUP

> 2 tablespoons shortening
> 3 onions, chopped
> 2 carrots, diced
> 2 pounds beef (flank or chuck)
> Beef bones
> ½ cup medium barley, washed
>   and drained
> 8½ cups water
> 2 teaspoons salt
> ½ teaspoon pepper

Melt the shortening in a saucepan. Sauté the onions and carrots in it for 10 minutes. Add the beef, bones, barley, water, salt, and pepper. Bring to a boil and cook over low heat for 2½ hours, or until meat and barley are tender.

Serve the soup with pieces of meat in it.

To some people this is just a soup, to me it's a thermometer. When My Jake was just starting in his business, for us to have this soup was a hardship, but since it was a favorite of one and all, a little hardship was sometimes a pleasure. The potatoes I had and onions were always in the house, but the lox (that's salmon) was a different story. To buy the best cut was not within my realm, so I had to make do with the end cuts. As My Jake progressed in the financial department, I graduated to the middle cuts. So I always knew the state of our finances because good times meant the center of the lox and the bad times meant the end cuts. What other kind of soup is such a financial wizard?

SMOKED SALMON SOUP

3 tablespoons butter
2 onions, chopped
2 tablespoons flour
5 cups water
1½ pounds halibut, cubed (or other white-meat fish)
½ teaspoon freshly ground black pepper
3 potatoes, peeled and cubed
1 cup heavy cream
6 slices smoked salmon
2 tablespoons chopped parsley

Melt the butter in a saucepan. Sauté the onions in it for 5 minutes, stirring frequently. Sprinkle with the flour, stirring until browned.

Add the water, stirring constantly until the boiling point. Add the fish and pepper. Cook over medium heat for 15 minutes. Add the potatoes, and cook for 20 minutes. Add the cream, stirring constantly. Add the smoked salmon and parsley, and cook for 2 minutes. Correct seasoning. No salt is provided in the recipe, as it will depend upon the saltiness of the salmon.

Serve in deep bowls.

BEEF SOUP

2 pounds beef (plate flank or
  breast flank)
Beef bones
2½ quarts water
1 onion
3 stalks celery
6 sprigs parsley
2 carrots, scraped
1 parsnip, scraped and cut in half
1 parsley root or celery root,
  scraped
1 tablespoon salt
¼ teaspoon freshly ground black
  pepper

Combine the beef, beef bones, water, and onion in a saucepan. Bring to a boil and skim the top. Cover and cook over medium heat for 1 hour. Add the celery, parsley, carrots, parsnip, parsley root, salt, and pepper. Cook over low heat for 1½ hours additional, or until the meat is very tender. Strain the soup and serve with any desired soup garnish.

The meat may be served separately with Beet Horseradish Salad.

Ptcha *is a food and not an error in spelling. In the fancy shops they call it calf's-foot jelly, but how many people can eat it from those little jars? To get enough to feed my family I would have to buy out the whole place. Confidentially and between us, what they sell in the store is seasoned sweet. Of course it's a matter of taste, but everybody likes my* ptcha. *So I make it at home with my little improvements and My Uncle David says my* ptcha *you couldn't buy anyplace, try as you may. Maybe my little improvements . . . Must be something.*

PTCHA

CALF'S-FOOT SOUP
AND JELLY

3 calf's feet (about 6 pounds), each cut into eighths by butcher
2 onions
3 cloves garlic
4 quarts water
1 tablespoon salt
1 teaspoon freshly ground black pepper
6 hard-cooked eggs
¼ cup cider vinegar
3 tablespoons sugar
4 cloves garlic, minced

Pour boiling water over the calf's feet. Scrape and scrub them thoroughly. Combine the calf's feet, onions, whole garlic, and water in a saucepan. Bring to a boil; skim the top. Cover, and cook over low

45

heat for 2 hours. Add the salt and ½ teaspoon of the pepper. Cover and cook for 2 hours longer, or until the meat separates from the bones. Correct seasoning. Strain, and separate the meat from the bones. Chop coarsely.

soup: Measure 6 cups of the stock, and place in a saucepan. Mash 3 of the eggs. Add the vinegar, sugar, and half of the minced garlic. Add to the soup, together with ½ of the meat. Heat. Correct seasoning. Serve with garlic toast.

jelly: Divide the remaining stock, meat, and minced garlic between 2 glass pie plates. Set aside for 30 minutes. Slice the remaining eggs, and arrange on top of the jelly. Sprinkle with the remaining pepper. Serve chilled, as an appetizer.

CHICKEN SOUP

1 6-pound chicken (pullet)
Chicken feet and giblets
2½ quarts water
1 onion
3 stalks celery
8 sprigs parsley
2 carrots, scraped
2 leeks
1 parsley root or celery root,
   scraped
1 tablespoon salt

Singe and wash the chicken thoroughly. Scrape the chicken feet. Combine the chicken, chicken feet, giblets, water, and onion in a saucepan. Bring to a boil. Skim the top. Cover and cook over medium heat for 1 hour. Add the celery, parsley, carrots, leeks, parsley root, and salt. Cook over low heat for 1½ hours longer, or until the chicken is tender. Strain the soup and serve with any desired soup garnish such as noodles, *kasha*, rice, etc.

The chicken may be served separately.

46

SAUERKRAUT FISH SOUP

3 tablespoons butter
2 onions, sliced
2 tablespoons flour
3 cups sauerkraut juice
3 cups water
2 carrots, sliced
1 stalk celery
2 tomatoes, chopped
2 teaspoons salt
½ teaspoon freshly ground black pepper
6 slices fish (pike, whitefish, or salmon trout)
3 potatoes, peeled and quartered
3 tablespoons chopped parsley
3 tablespoons chopped dill
2 egg yolks
½ cup sour cream

Melt the butter in a saucepan. Sauté the onions in it for 10 minutes, stirring frequently. Sprinkle with the flour, stirring until smooth. Add the sauerkraut juice and water, stirring constantly. Add the carrots, celery, tomatoes, salt, and pepper. Bring to a boil and cook over medium heat for 20 minutes. Add the fish, potatoes, parsley, and dill. Cook over low heat for 35 minutes. Discard the celery.

Beat the egg yolks and sour cream together. Add 1 cup of the stock, beating constantly to prevent curdling. Return the mixture to the saucepan, mixing well. Correct seasoning.

Serve hot or cold in deep soup plates.

This recipe was passed down to me from Mrs. Barnett, who lives upstairs in 6E. By me it's potato soup and by her it's vichyssoise (that's French). How it got so fancy I don't know, but if Mrs. Barnett likes her potato soup French and I like mine plain, what's the difference? It tastes the same and a name is only a name. So I don't mind at all what Mrs. Barnett calls her soup because she's Dora's mother and My Sammy and Dora are going steady together. A good soup is only soup but Dora could be a daughter-in-law, and I ask you, what's more important? Anyway, try this soup, hot or cold, it's good, and French or English, it's also good.

MRS. BARNETT'S
CREAMED POTATO SOUP

4 tablespoons butter
4 leeks, or 2 onions, sliced
3 potatoes, peeled and sliced
2 tablespoons fine barley, presoaked (optional)
1 stalk celery
2 sprigs parsley
2 teaspoons salt
¼ teaspoon freshly ground black
   pepper
6 cups water
1 cup light cream

Melt the butter in a saucepan. Add the leeks; cook over low heat for 10 minutes, but do not allow them to brown. Add the potatoes, barley, celery, parsley, salt, pepper, and water. Cook over low heat for 30 minutes. Discard the celery and parsley. Add the cream. Correct seasoning. Heat, and serve.

If a smooth soup is desired, purée the soup in a food mill or an electric blender.

MEAT BALL SOUP

6 cups water
2 beef bones
2 onions, chopped
1 carrot, sliced
1 celery root, peeled and diced
1 tomato, chopped
2 cups sauerkraut juice
2 tablespoons chopped parsley
2 tablespoons chopped dill
3 teaspoons salt
½ teaspoon freshly ground black pepper
1 pound ground beef
6 tablespoons rice
1 egg
½ cup flour
2 egg yolks

Combine the water, beef bones, onions, carrot, celery root, and tomato in a saucepan. Bring to a boil and cook over medium heat for 1½ hours. Strain and return to the saucepan. Add the sauerkraut juice, parsley, dill, 2 teaspoons of the salt, and ¼ teaspoon of the pepper. Bring to a boil and cook over medium heat while preparing the meat balls.

Mix the beef, 2 tablespoons of the rice, the egg, and remaining salt and pepper together. Shape into ½-inch balls. Roll in the flour. Add the remaining rice to the soup. Add the meat balls. Cook over medium heat for 20 minutes.

Beat the egg yolks in a bowl. Gradually add 2 cups of the soup, beating constantly to prevent curdling. Return the mixture to the balance of the soup, mixing steadily.

Reheat, but do not allow to boil.

NOTE: If desired, canned consommé can replace the home-made beef-bone stock.

FISH BORSCHT

BEET, CABBAGE, AND
FISH SOUP

4 tablespoons shortening
2 onions, chopped
1 head (about 2 pounds)
    cabbage, shredded
½ pound mushrooms, sliced
4 beets, peeled and grated
7 cups water
3½ teaspoons salt
½ teaspoon freshly ground black
    pepper
1 bay leaf
2 tablespoons lemon juice
1 teaspoon sugar
1 cup bread crumbs
6 fillets of fish (carp, whitefish,
    or sole)

Melt 1 tablespoon of the shortening in a saucepan. Sauté the onions in it for 10 minutes, stirring frequently. Add the cabbage, mushrooms, beets, water, 2½ teaspoons of the salt, ¼ teaspoon of the pepper, the bay leaf, lemon juice, and sugar. Bring to a boil and cook over medium heat for 1 hour. Correct seasoning. Discard the bay leaf.

Combine the bread crumbs with the remaining salt and pepper. Dip the fish into the bread crumbs.

Melt the remaining shortening in a skillet. Fry the fish in it until browned on both sides and done.

Place a piece of fish in each soup plate, and pour the soup over it.

FARINA SOUP

3 tablespoons shortening
1 cup farina
6 cups stock or canned
    consommé
¼ teaspoon freshly ground black
    pepper

Melt the shortening in a skillet. Add the farina. Cook over low heat until browned, stirring constantly.

Bring the stock to a boil in a saucepan. Add the farina, stirring constantly. Add the pepper. Cook over low heat for 5 minutes. Correct seasoning.

RYE-BREAD SOUP

2 tablespoons butter
2 onions, chopped
5 potatoes, peeled and cubed
6 cups water
5 slices rye bread, trimmed, cut
    into cubes
1 bay leaf
2 stalks celery
4 sprigs parsley
2 teaspoons salt
½ teaspoon freshly ground black
    pepper
1 cup sour cream
1 egg yolk

Melt the butter in a saucepan. Add the onions. Sauté for 10 minutes, stirring frequently. Add the potatoes and water. Cook over low heat for 10 minutes. Add the bread, bay leaf, celery, parsley, salt, and pepper. Cook over low heat for 20 minutes. Discard the bay leaf, celery, and parsley. Purée the mixture in an electric blender or force the mixture through a sieve.

Beat the cream and egg yolk together in a bowl. Add 2 cups of the soup gradually, stirring constantly to prevent curdling. Return the mixture to the balance of the soup. Reheat, but do not allow to boil. Correct seasoning and serve.

Fish

Fish is a brain food, at least that's what everybody told me when I was a girl. I don't know what's the truth behind such a story, but for some people maybe it is. Fish is one of my favorites and I'm not any smarter than I ever was, but for My Uncle David's Solly the Doctor the story is different. Fish is his favorite food, and smart he is. The fish recipes that I have here are the ones I like the best, and if you like them too it will prove that if I'm not so smart at least I know what's good. That's also important.

TANTE ELKA'S FISH

¼ cup olive oil
6 onions, sliced
2½ teaspoons salt
½ teaspoon freshly ground black
  pepper
6 slices fish (carp, pike, or
  salmon)
⅓ cup water
1 tablespoon vinegar
1 tablespoon sugar
1 bay leaf
2 lemons, sliced thin
2 tomatoes, peeled and sliced
2 tablespoons chopped parsley

Heat the olive oil in a skillet. Add the onions. Sauté for 10 minutes, stirring frequently. Sprinkle the salt and pepper over the fish. Arrange the fish on top of the onions.

Mix the water, vinegar, and sugar together and pour over the fish. Add the bay leaf and lemon slices. Cover and cook over low heat for 20 minutes. Add the tomatoes and parsley and cook for 20 minutes longer. Correct seasoning.

Serve cold.

Sometimes when time grows heavy on my hands and I have nothing to do I make this pickled fish. Why? Because in my house who knows who will fall in and visit, and if the unexpected comes by, what will I feed them? I mean it's not a visit unless you can have a little something, so the pickled fish is good. You can make it in your leisure and keep it in the Frigidator. It will stay there for two weeks at least, and you mean to say that in two weeks nobody will call? Don't be foolish.

PICKLED FISH

6 onions, sliced
12 thin slices fish (salmon, pike,
    or whitefish)
2½ teaspoons salt
½ teaspoon freshly ground black
    pepper
3 cups water
¾ cup white vinegar
2 tablespoons sugar
2 teaspoons pickling spice
2 bay leaves

Place 3 of the onions on the bottom of a saucepan. Arrange the fish over it. Add the salt, pepper, and water. Bring to a boil. Cook over low heat for 35 minutes.

Arrange alternate layers of the fish and remaining onions in a bowl or jar. Combine the stock, vinegar, sugar, pickling spice, and bay leaves. Bring to a boil. Pour over the fish.

Allow to marinate in the refrigerator for at least 2 days before serving. The jellied fish will keep for about 2 weeks in the refrigerator.

PICKLED FRIED FISH

⅓ cup flour
2 teaspoons salt
¼ teaspoon pepper
6 slices fish (pike, whitefish, or
    sole)
4 tablespoons shortening
1 cup vinegar
2 onions, sliced thin
2 bay leaves
¼ teaspoon pickling spice
4 peppercorns
1 tablespoon sugar
1 lemon, sliced
1 tablespoon olive oil

Mix the flour, salt, and pepper together. Dip the fish in this mixture lightly. Melt the shortening; fry the fish in it until browned on both sides. Place in a bowl or jar.

Combine the vinegar, onions, bay leaves, pickling spice, peppercorns, and sugar in a saucepan. Bring to a boil and cook over low heat for 10 minutes. Add the lemon and oil and pour over the fish. Cover and let marinate in the refrigerator for at least 12 hours.

The fish will keep for a week or more.

FRIED MACKEREL

½ cup flour
3 teaspoons salt
½ teaspoon pepper
6 fillets of mackerel
4 tablespoons butter
1 onion, chopped
¼ pound mushrooms, chopped
2 tablespoons lemon juice

57

Mix the flour, 2 teaspoons salt, and ¼ teaspoon pepper together. Dip the fillets in this mixture. Melt 2 tablespoons of the butter in a skillet. Fry the fish in it until browned on both sides. Remove fish and keep warm. Melt remaining butter in the skillet. Sauté the onion and mushrooms in it for 10 minutes. Add the lemon juice and remaining salt and pepper. Cook 1 minute. Pour over fish and serve.

JELLIED CARP WITH GRAPES

4 tablespoons olive oil
2 onions, chopped
2 cups boiling water
1 cup dry white wine
2½ teaspoons salt
½ teaspoon freshly ground black
  pepper
1 bay leaf
6 slices carp
⅛ teaspoon saffron
2 teaspoons gelatin
3 tablespoons cold water
1 cup seedless grapes

Heat the olive oil in a saucepan. Sauté the onions in it for 10 minutes, stirring frequently. Add the water, wine, salt, pepper, and bay leaf. Bring to a boil; carefully place the fish in it. Cover and cook over low heat for 45 minutes. Carefully transfer the fish to a serving platter.

Dissolve the saffron in the fish stock. Soften the gelatin in the cold water for 5 minutes and add to the stock, stirring until dissolved. Correct seasoning and discard bay leaf. Arrange the grapes around the fish and pour the stock over it. Chill until jellied.

Some people you can teach and some people you can't. Dora makes gefilte fish like nobody. She used to come to my house to be with Sammy. They had a crunch on each other, and between the comings and the goings and the excuses for Dora to come down by us, I showed her how to make gefilte fish. Listen, one excuse is as good as another. So Dora learned how to make fish and with her own improvements on the recipe it's out of this world. Sammy says she makes the best gefilte fish and I know that Love can be blind, but the appetite is a different story altogether, and My Sammy knows whereof without a doubt.

DORA'S GEFILTE FISH

CHOPPED FISH BALLS

4 pounds fish fillets (whitefish, pike, or other fresh-water fish —use 2 varieties if possible)
Head and skin of fish
5 onions
4 teaspoons salt
1½ teaspoons white pepper
1 teaspoon sugar
2 eggs, beaten
5½ cups water
3 tablespoons cracker or matzo meal
2 carrots, sliced

Grind the fish and 1 onion in a food chopper. Place in a wooden bowl; add 2 teaspoons of the salt, ¾ teaspoon of the pepper, the sugar, eggs, ½ cup of the water, and the cracker meal. Chop until fine in texture and well blended.

Place the fish head and skin in a deep saucepan. Slice the remaining onions and place over them. Add the carrots, remaining water, and remaining salt and pepper. Bring to an active boil. Shape the chopped fish into 2-inch balls between wet hands. Carefully drop them into the saucepan. Cover and cook over low heat for 1½ hours. Shake the saucepan frequently. Correct seasoning.

Remove the fish balls carefully. Strain the stock into a separate bowl and chill until jellied. Serve the cold fish and the jelly with fresh horseradish.

FISH WITH EGG SAUCE

1 tablespoon salt
¼ teaspoon white pepper
6 slices fish (lake trout, whitefish, or pike)
3 onions, sliced
2 carrots, scraped and sliced
2 stalks celery, sliced
1 parsley root, cubed
2 cups water
3 tablespoons ground blanched almonds
2 egg yolks
2 tablespoons chopped parsley

Mix the salt and pepper together and rub into the fish. Place the onions, carrots, celery, and parsley root in a saucepan. Arrange the fish over the vegetables; add the water. Bring to a boil and cook over low heat 45 minutes. Place the fish on a platter. Force the stock and vegetables through a sieve or purée in an electric blender. Add the almonds.

Beat the egg yolks in a saucepan. Gradually add the stock, beating constantly to prevent curdling. Reheat, but do not allow to boil. Pour over the fish. Sprinkle with parsley and serve.

This recipe is special. Special because to work out the exact ingredients was a job for My Uncle David. Why David? Well, he has an ear for Sweet and Sour Fish. I wouldn't make it without David's assistance to taste it every step of the way. And when we put the recipe on paper I insisted that David stand by with me, and what you have here is the guaranteed Sweet and Sour Fish like I always make according to Uncle David.

SWEET AND SOUR FISH

1½ cups vinegar
¾ cup water
⅓ cup sugar
2 teaspoons salt
3 tablespoons butter (optional)
4 onions, sliced
2 lemons, sliced
6 slices fish (salmon, whitefish,
   lake trout, or pike)
¾ cup seedless raisins
¼ cup blanched almonds, sliced
2 egg yolks

Combine the vinegar, water, sugar, salt, and butter in a saucepan. Boil for 5 minutes. Add the onions, lemons, and fish. Cook over low heat for 15 minutes. Add the raisins and almonds. Cover and cook over low heat for 35 minutes. Remove the fish to a platter. Discard the lemon slices.

Beat the egg yolks in a bowl. Gradually add the fish stock, beating constantly to prevent curdling. Pour the sauce over the fish. Chill for several hours.

CANNED SALMON CROQUETTES

2 cans (7¾ ounces) salmon
¼ teaspoon pepper
4 tablespoons grated onion
2 eggs
2 teaspoons lemon juice
¾ cup bread crumbs
4 tablespoons shortening

Drain and mash the salmon. Add the pepper, onion, eggs, lemon juice, and 3 tablespoons bread crumbs. Mix well. Shape into croquettes and dip lightly in remaining bread crumbs.

Heat the shortening in a skillet. Fry the croquettes in it over medium heat until browned on both sides.

SAUERKRAUT-STUFFED FISH

3 teaspoons salt
¾ teaspoon freshly ground black pepper
4 pounds fish, split for stuffing (whitefish, salmon, trout, or sea bass)
1½ pounds sauerkraut
½ cup shortening
2 onions
1 apple, peeled and grated
2 tablespoons flour

Mix 2 teaspoons of the salt and ½ teaspoon of the pepper together, and sprinkle on the fish.

Cover the sauerkraut with water in a saucepan; bring to a boil and cook over medium heat for 10 minutes. Drain well.

Melt 2 tablespoons of the shortening in a skillet. Add the onions and sauté for 10 minutes, stirring frequently. Add the sauerkraut and remaining salt and pepper. Cook over medium heat for 5 minutes, stirring almost constantly. Add the apple and mix well. Stuff the fish with the mixture. Sew or fasten the opening with skewers or toothpicks. Sprinkle flour on the fish.

Melt the remaining shortening in a baking dish. Place the fish in it. Bake in a 375° oven for 1 hour, basting frequently.

BAKED FISH DUMPLINGS

2 slices white bread, trimmed
½ cup boiling water
4 tablespoons butter
1 onion, chopped
2 pounds fillet of white-meat fish
   (halibut, whitefish, or pike)
3 teaspoons salt
½ teaspoon white pepper
2 egg yolks
3 tablespoons cold water
2 onions, sliced
3 tomatoes, chopped
2 tablespoons chopped parsley

Soak the bread in the boiling water for 5 minutes. Drain and mash.

Melt 2 tablespoons of the butter in a skillet. Sauté the chopped onion in it for 5 minutes. Add the bread; sauté 2 minutes. Grind or chop the fish very fine. Add the onion mixture, 2 teaspoons salt, ¼ teaspoon pepper, the egg yolks, and cold water. Chop until well blended and smooth. Shape into 2-inch balls.

Melt the remaining butter in a baking dish. Add the sliced onions, tomatoes, remaining salt and pepper, and the fish balls.

Bake in a 350° oven for 35 minutes, basting frequently and adding a little water if necessary. Sprinkle with the parsley and serve.

MACKEREL CROQUETTES

¼ pound butter
3 onions, chopped
3 pounds mackerel fillets
1 clove garlic, minced
2 teaspoons salt
½ teaspoon freshly ground black
   pepper
½ teaspoon sugar
2 eggs, beaten
3 tablespoons cold water

Melt half the butter in a skillet. Sauté the onions in it until brown. Grind the fish in a food chopper or chop it in a wooden bowl. Add the onions, garlic, salt, pepper, and sugar. Chop or grind until smooth and well blended. Add the eggs and water. Mix well.

Melt the remaining butter in a skillet. Between wet hands, shape the croquettes into the desired size. Fry over low heat until browned on both sides.

Serve hot or cold. Very small croquettes make a delicious *hors d'oeuvre*, particularly when served with a little English mustard.

PAPRIKA FISH

4 tablespoons butter
4 onions, chopped
2 teaspoons paprika
6 slices fish (pike, whitefish, or
   sea bass)
2 teaspoons salt
½ teaspoon freshly ground black
   pepper
1 cup water
½ cup sour cream

Melt the shortening in a saucepan. Add the onions. Sauté for 10 minutes, stirring frequently. Add the paprika and mix well. Arrange the fish over the onions. Sprinkle with the salt and pepper. Add the water and bring to a boil. Cover and cook over low heat for 45 minutes. Correct seasoning. Carefully remove the fish to a platter.

Add the sour cream to the sauce, mixing constantly. Heat, but do not allow to boil. Pour the sauce over the fish and serve.

SMOKED SALMON AND POTATO KUGEL (PUDDING)

4 tablespoons butter
2 onions, chopped
5 potatoes, peeled
¼ teaspoon freshly ground black pepper
6 slices smoked salmon
2 eggs
1 teaspoon salt
1 cup light cream
½ cup milk

Melt the butter in a skillet. Sauté the onions in it for 10 minutes, stirring frequently.

Preheat oven to 325°. Slice the potatoes as thin as possible. In a buttered casserole arrange successive layers of potatoes, sprinkled with pepper, and the smoked salmon and sautéed onions. Start and end with the potatoes.

Beat the eggs, salt, cream, and milk together. Pour over the potatoes.

Bake for 50 minutes, or until set and lightly browned on top.

Serve as a luncheon or supper dish.

BAKED STUFFED FISH

3 teaspoons salt
½ teaspoon pepper
1 3- to 4-pound fish (whitefish,
    pike, lake trout), split for
    stuffing
1½ cups bread crumbs
¾ cup milk
1 onion, grated
½ cup melted butter
½ cup corn meal
½ cup light cream

Mix 2 teaspoons of the salt and pepper together; rub into the fish. Mix bread crumbs, milk, onion, and 3 tablespoons of the melted butter and remaining salt together, and stuff the fish. Fasten the opening with skewers, toothpicks, or thread. Roll the fish in the corn meal.

Pour the remaining butter into a baking dish; place fish in it.

Bake in a 350° oven 20 minutes. Add cream and bake 30 minutes longer, basting frequently.

COLD BOILED FISH

4 onions, sliced
1 stalk celery, sliced
2 carrots, sliced
6 slices fish (whitefish, pike, or
    carp)
2 teaspoons salt
½ teaspoon freshly ground black
    pepper
¼ teaspoon sugar
2 cups water

Place the onions, celery, and carrots on the bottom of a saucepan.

Arrange the fish over them. Add the salt, pepper, sugar, and water. Bring to a boil. Cover and cook over low heat for 50 minutes.

Carefully remove the fish to a platter. Pour the stock over it. Chill for at least 4 hours.

This is a dish a king would like. And why not? Pike is a wonderful fish, and noodles? Noodles are my downfall, so when you put them together how wrong could it be? Try it and I'm sure you'll be an attic with me.

PIKE WITH NOODLES

4 slices pike (about 2 pounds)
  or similar fish
2 cups water
2 onions, sliced
3 teaspoons salt
2 teaspoons pepper
¼ pound butter
1 package (8 ounces) broad
  noodles, half cooked
3 tablespoons flour
1 cup light cream
½ cup grated gruyère cheese

Wash the fish thoroughly. Combine in a saucepan with the water, onions, 2 teaspoons of the salt, and 1 teaspoon of the pepper. Cook over medium heat for 35 minutes. Remove the fish from the stock and allow to cool. Strain the stock and reserve 1 cup. Remove the skin and bones from the fish, and flake the fish finely.

Melt half the butter in a saucepan. Add the half-cooked noodles and sauté for 10 minutes, stirring frequently. Add the fish and mix together lightly.

Melt the remaining butter in a saucepan. Add the flour and stir until very smooth. Add the reserved cup of stock and the cream, stirring constantly until the boiling point. Cook over low heat for 5 minutes. Add the remaining salt, pepper, and the cheese. Stir until the cheese is melted. Preheat oven to 425°.

Place the noodle-and-fish mixture in a buttered casserole. Pour the sauce over it. Bake for 20 minutes.

Serve hot.

NOTE: This is an excellent dish for using up leftover fish. If fish stock is not available, substitute 1 cup of milk in its place.

FISH IN SOUR CREAM

6 tablespoons butter
1 onion, grated
2 eggs
1½ teaspoons salt
½ teaspoon freshly ground black
    pepper
¼ teaspoon dry mustard
6 fish fillets (flounder, sole, or
    whitefish)
1 cup bread crumbs
1 cup sour cream
2 tablespoons chopped parsley

Melt 2 tablespoons of the butter in a skillet. Add the onion. Sauté for 5 minutes, stirring frequently. Cool.

Beat the eggs, salt, pepper, mustard, and sautéed onion together. Dip the fish in this mixture and then in the bread crumbs, coating both sides.

Melt the remaining butter in a skillet. Fry the fish in it for 5 minutes on each side. Add the sour cream; cook over low heat for 10 minutes. Sprinkle with the parsley and serve.

BAKED FISH AND VEGETABLES

½ cup olive or salad oil
2 potatoes, peeled and diced
2 carrots, sliced
½ pound fresh green peas, or
    ¼ package frozen peas
1 green pepper, sliced thin
2 onions, chopped
2 cloves garlic, minced
3 teaspoons salt
1 teaspoon freshly ground black
    pepper
1 bay leaf
6 slices fish (carp, whitefish, or
    halibut)

Bring the oil to a boil in a deep casserole. Add the potatoes, carrots, peas, green pepper, onions, garlic, 1½ teaspoons of the salt, ½ teaspoon of the pepper, and the bay leaf. Mix together. Cook over low heat for 20 minutes. Preheat oven to 350°.

Sprinkle the remaining salt and pepper over the fish. Place the fish over the vegetables.

Bake for 35 minutes, or until the fish is browned. Remove the bay leaf and serve.

HERRING PUDDING

4 fillets salt herring
4 potatoes, peeled and boiled
2 eggs
4 tablespoons sour cream
¼ teaspoon freshly ground black
    pepper

Soak the herring in water to cover overnight. Change the water at least twice. Drain well.

Chop the herring very fine. Mash the potatoes. Beat the herring, potatoes, eggs, sour cream, and pepper together until smooth and light. Pour into a buttered casserole or baking dish.

Bake in a 425° oven for 25 minutes, or until delicately browned.

Serve with a green vegetable as a complete lunch, or serve as a light supper dish.

HERRING CROQUETTES

3 salt herring
¼ pound butter
1 onion, chopped
1 cup bread crumbs
1 egg, beaten
⅛ teaspoon freshly ground black pepper

Wash the herring thoroughly. Soak them overnight in water to cover, changing the water several times. Remove the skin and bones carefully. Chop the herring fine.

Melt 3 tablespoons of the butter in a skillet. Add the onion and sauté for 10 minutes, stirring frequently. Add ½ cup of the bread crumbs. Cook for 15 minutes, stirring occasionally. Remove from the heat. Add the egg, pepper, and chopped herring and mix well. Shape into croquettes of any desired size and dip them in the remaining bread crumbs.

Melt the remaining butter in a skillet. Fry the croquettes until brown on both sides. Serve with boiled potatoes.

Poultry

How many different chickens are there? There's turkey and goose and duck, there's grouse and pheasant and capons and squabs, guinea hens and quail. So what can you do with all these fowls? You can roast them, boil them, fry them, fricassee them, and with the leftovers you can make a stew or sandwiches. So what can you do with anything else? There's only a few ways to cook anything and my grandmother used to say, "What you put in you take out." True, very true. It's what you put in that makes the difference. These are my favorite recipes for poultry, and if you try them I'm sure you'll like them too.

ROAST DUCK
PINCUS PINES STYLE

2 cloves garlic, minced
4 teaspoons salt
1 teaspoon freshly ground black
  pepper
2 teaspoons paprika
1 6-pound duck
4 tablespoons shortening
2 onions, chopped
½ pound broad noodles, cooked
  and drained
3 tablespoons bread crumbs
2 tablespoons chopped parsley
2 eggs

Mix the garlic, 3 teaspoons of the salt, ½ teaspoon of the pepper, and the paprika to a paste. Rub into the duck, inside and out.

Melt the shortening in a skillet. Sauté the onions in it for 10 minutes, stirring frequently. Mix the noodles, bread crumbs, parsley, eggs, sautéed onions, and remaining salt and pepper together. Stuff the duck. Fasten the opening with skewers or cover with aluminum foil. Place in a roasting pan.

Roast in a 400° oven for 30 minutes. Pour off the fat. Reduce heat to 350° and continue roasting for 2 hours additional, or until the duck is tender and crisp. Pour off the fat frequently while roasting.

When my Cousin Herman was a pfc in the army he married a French war bride from France. He wrote me that he wanted her to learn to cook like Cousin Molly when she arrived in the New World. So when she arrived and we discussed the cooking of this and that, my dear cousin-in-law taught me this recipe for duck for when you're expecting company. To Herman it was a revelation. If you try it, maybe it will open your eyes to a new delicacy from across the waves.

DENISE'S COMPANY DUCK

1 6-pound duck, disjointed
2 teaspoons salt
½ teaspoon pepper
1 clove garlic, minced
1 bay leaf
2 tomatoes, chopped
½ cup dry red wine
3 tablespoons brandy
½ pound mushrooms, sliced
6 green olives, sliced
6 ripe olives, sliced
2 tablespoons chopped parsley

Remove as much fat as possible from the duck. Combine the salt, pepper, and garlic and rub into the duck. Place in a hot skillet and brown well on all sides. Pour off the fat. Add the bay leaf, tomatoes, wine, and brandy. Cover and cook over low heat for 1½ hours. Skim fat. Add the mushrooms, olives, and parsley; cook 15 minutes.

ROAST STUFFED GOOSE

3 cloves garlic, minced
5 teaspoons salt
1¼ teaspoons freshly ground
    black pepper
2 teaspoons paprika
1 12- to 15-pound goose
4 tablespoons shortening
3 onions, chopped
½ pound mushrooms, chopped
¼ pound chicken livers, chopped
4 cups cooked buckwheat groats
    (*see page 207*)

Mix the garlic, 4 teaspoons of the salt, ¾ teaspoon of the pepper, and the paprika to a paste. Rub into the goose, inside and out.

Melt the shortening in a skillet. Add the onions and mushrooms. Sauté for 10 minutes, stirring frequently. Add the livers and sauté for 5 minutes longer. Add the groats and remaining salt and pepper. Mix lightly. Stuff the goose with the mixture.

Place the goose in a roasting pan. Roast in a 425° oven for 30 minutes. Pour off the fat. Prick the goose skin in several places with a fork. Reduce heat to 350° and roast for 2½ hours additional, or until goose is tender, crisp, and brown. Pour off the fat frequently while roasting.

To cook a goose is easy but it's an event. There is a reason why the goose is a bird that people save for celebrations, and when you taste it you'll know why. But the goose by itself is only a bird, but with stuffed helzel and crisp greben it's a feast. When my mother cooked a goose it was the talk of the village. Relatives would come from miles around to eat it and they would bring all their friends. My mother, a kindhearted woman, would never say no to anybody that happened to drop in. So when my father went to buy the goose he knew better than to get only one—two or three he always brought home because he knew what would happen when my mother started to cook. He would mumble and grumble about the extra people, but when my mother cooked he was the proudest man in the village. This is the recipe. It's guaranteed for a full house.

FRICASSEE OF GOOSE, GOOSE GREBEN (CRACKLINGS) AND STUFFED GOOSE NECK

1 12- to 15-pound goose, disjointed
2½ teaspoons salt
½ teaspoon freshly ground black pepper
2 teaspoons paprika
2 cloves garlic, minced
3 onions, chopped

Clean the goose, singeing the skin carefully. Make sure that no feathers remain. Remove as much skin as possible from the goose by slipping a sharp knife under it. Keep the skin of the neck intact. Reserve all the skin and fat of the goose.

Mix the salt, pepper, paprika, and garlic to a smooth paste. Rub it into the goose thoroughly. Measure ¼ cup of the goose fat and melt it in a Dutch oven or heavy saucepan. Add the onions and goose. Cover and cook over low heat for 3 hours, turning the goose frequently and adding a little boiling water if necessary.

GOOSE GREBEN

Fat, and skin of goose
2 onions, chopped

Cut the fat and skin into 1-inch pieces. Dry thoroughly. Place in a skillet and melt over low heat. When the fat is almost completely melted, add the onions. Continue cooking until the onions brown, stirring occasionally.

Strain the fat into containers; cover and store in the refrigerator. The fat may be used in cooking, with chopped chicken livers or chopped eggs, or it may be spread on bread. The *greben* may be eaten as an *hors d'oeuvre*.

STUFFED GOOSE NECK

1½ cups sifted flour
1½ teaspoons salt
½ teaspoon freshly ground black
    pepper
1½ teaspoons paprika
1 onion, grated
⅓ cup rendered goose fat

Mix together the flour, salt, pepper, paprika, onion, and goose fat. Sew the neck at one end with white thread. Stuff it with the mixture and sew the other end. Place it in the saucepan with the fricassee, above, for 2 hours. Slice, and serve with the goose.

GIBLETS 19 lb

BROILERS 49 lb

DUCKS 33 lb

I'm very lucky because twice a year, if I need the excuse, I can have turkey for a regular Thanksgiving meal. Once for Succoth and once for Thanksgiving. Succoth is the old Hebrew Festival of the Tabernacles and it also is a harvest celebration like Thanksgiving, where memories of the past and hope for the future mingle all together.

STUFFED TURKEY

4 teaspoons salt
1 teaspoon freshly ground black pepper
2 teaspoons paprika
2 cloves garlic, minced
1 12- to 14-pound turkey
Liver and gizzard of turkey
4 tablespoons shortening
2 onions, chopped
½ pound mushrooms, sliced
3 cups cooked brown rice

Mix 3 teaspoons of the salt, ¾ teaspoon of the pepper, the paprika, and garlic together. Rub into the turkey, inside and out. Grind the liver and gizzard in a food mill or chopper and set aside.

Melt the shortening in a skillet. Add the onions. Sauté for 10 minutes, stirring frequently. Add the mushrooms. Sauté for 5 minutes. Remove the onions and mushrooms and set aside. Sauté the liver and gizzard for 5 minutes. Combine the brown rice, onions, mushrooms, liver, gizzard, and remaining salt and pepper. Mix well. Stuff the turkey, closing the opening with skewers, thread, or aluminum foil. Place in a roasting pan.

Roast in a 350° oven for 2½ hours, or until the turkey is tender. Baste frequently with the pan juices.

TURKEY DISH FOR
LADIES' AID SOCIETY

4 tablespoons shortening
2 onions, chopped
1 green pepper, coarsely chopped
2 stalks celery, sliced
½ pound mushrooms, sliced
2 tablespoons flour
1½ cups chicken stock or canned
    consommé
1½ teaspoons salt
¼ teaspoon freshly ground black
    pepper
3 cups diced cooked turkey or
    chicken
1 cup green peas, cooked or
    canned
2 tablespoons chopped parsley
6 slices toast

Melt the shortening in a saucepan. Add the onions, green pepper, celery, and mushrooms. Sauté for 15 minutes, stirring frequently. All the liquid should be evaporated. Sprinkle with the flour, stirring until smooth and brown. Add the stock, stirring constantly until the boiling point. Add the salt, pepper, turkey, green peas, and parsley. Stir. Cook over low heat for 10 minutes. Correct seasoning.

Pour over the toast and serve.

Whenever I have fried chicken at my table I always tell everyone to pick up the chicken in their fingers. After all, like I always say, fingers were made before forks, and hands before knives. If you don't eat chicken with your fingers you lose half the flavor. When we have company that's extra polite and the chicken is sitting and they won't use their fingers, I give Jake a look and Jake gives me a look and then he picks up the chicken leg or whatever and eats. The hint is very soon taken by one and all, and before you know it the stranger in the house is an old friend.

BAKED FRIED CHICKEN AUSTRIAN STYLE

1 cup sifted flour
2 teaspoons salt
½ teaspoon freshly ground black pepper
1 teaspoon paprika
2 3½-pound chickens, disjointed
2 eggs, beaten
2 tablespoons water
2 cups cracker meal or matzo meal
½ cup shortening
3 onions, chopped

Mix the flour, salt, pepper, and paprika together. Roll the chicken in flour mixture. Combine the eggs and water. Dip the chicken in egg mixture, then in the cracker meal, coating the pieces heavily.

Heat half of the shortening in a skillet. Brown the chicken in it over low heat on all sides, adding more shortening as necessary. Transfer the pieces to a baking dish as they are browned. Sauté the onions for 10 minutes in the fat remaining in the skillet, stirring frequently. Place the onions over the chicken.

Bake in a 350° oven for 45 minutes, or until the chicken is tender.

BAKED BROILERS

3 broilers, halved
½ cup lemon juice
2½ teaspoons salt
1 tablespoon powdered ginger
1 clove garlic, minced
2 onions, sliced thin
½ cup melted shortening

Sponge the broilers with the lemon juice.

Combine the salt, ginger, and garlic. Rub the mixture into the broilers and set aside for 2 or more hours, if possible.

Place the broilers in a greased baking pan. Arrange the sliced onions on top, and pour the shortening over them.

Bake in a 400° oven for 45 minutes, or until browned and tender. Baste frequently.

CHICKEN PATTIES

2 tablespoons shortening
1 onion, chopped
2 slices white bread
⅓ cup hot water
3 cups ground cooked chicken
1 teaspoon salt
¼ teaspoon white pepper
2 egg yolks
2 egg whites, stiffly beaten
Fat for deep frying

Heat the shortening in a skillet. Sauté the onion for 10 minutes. Soak the bread in the water, and mash until smooth. Grind or chop together the chicken, sautéed onion, and bread. Add the salt, pepper, and egg yolks, mixing well. Fold in the egg whites.

Heat the fat to 375°; drop the mixture into it by the tablespoon. Fry until delicately browned. Drain.

GIBLET FRICASSEE

2 tablespoons flour
4 tablespoons shortening
3 onions, chopped
1½ cups boiling water
4 chicken gizzards
4 chicken necks
6 chicken wings
6 chicken feet, peeled and
  scraped
1 pound ground beef
1 egg
3 tablespoons bread crumbs
1 clove garlic, minced
2½ teaspoons salt
½ teaspoon freshly ground black
  pepper

Brown the flour in a skillet, stirring constantly to prevent burning.

Melt the shortening in a saucepan. Add the onions. Sauté for 15 minutes, stirring frequently. Sprinkle with the flour, stirring until smooth. Add the boiling water, stirring constantly until the boiling point. Add the gizzards, necks, wings, and feet. Cover and cook over low heat for 1 hour.

Mix the beef, egg, bread crumbs, garlic, 1 teaspoon of the salt, and ¼ teaspoon of the pepper. Shape into walnut-sized balls. Drop into the fricassee. Add remaining salt and pepper. Cook for 30 minutes additional.

Serve with boiled rice.

CHICKEN AND EGG-BARLEY HASH

3 tablespoons shortening
2 onions, chopped
2 cups diced cooked chicken
3 cups cooked egg barley
1½ teaspoons salt
½ teaspoon
    black pepper
½ teaspoon paprika
2 tablespoons chopped parsley

Melt the shortening in a skillet. Sauté the onions in it for 10 minutes. Add the chicken, egg barley, salt, pepper, paprika, and parsley. Sauté for 10 minutes, or until browned.

CHICKEN LIVER PIE

1½ pounds chicken livers
6 tablespoons shortening
2 onions, sliced thin
½ pound mushrooms, sliced
3 teaspoons salt
¾ teaspoon pepper
5 potatoes, peeled and sliced thin
2 cups shelled green peas, fresh or
    frozen
2 egg yolks
3 tablespoons Madeira wine

Wash the livers thoroughly and remove any discolored parts. Melt half the shortening in a skillet. Sauté the livers, onions, and mushrooms for 10 minutes, stirring occasionally. Drain if any liquid remains. Add 1½ teaspoons of salt and ½ teaspoon of pepper.

In a deep 11-inch greased pie plate arrange as many layers as possible of the potatoes sprinkled with some of the remaining salt and pepper, the liver mixture, and the peas. Start and end with the potatoes. Dot with the remaining shortening. Preheat the oven to 350°.

Beat the egg yolks and Madeira wine together and pour over the top layer of potatoes.

Bake 40 minutes or until the potatoes are browned and tender. Serve directly from the pie plate.

CHICKEN AND PEPPERS

2 teaspoons salt
½ teaspoon pepper
3 tablespoons flour
2 2½-pound chickens, disjointed
¼ cup olive oil
2 onions, chopped
2 cloves garlic, minced
3 tomatoes, peeled and chopped
4 green peppers, cut into eighths
2 tablespoons chopped parsley

Combine the salt, pepper, and flour. Lightly dust the chicken with the mixture.

Heat olive oil in a deep skillet. Sauté onions and garlic in it for 5 minutes. Add chicken and brown well. Add tomatoes and green peppers. Cover and cook over low heat for 45 minutes, or until chicken is tender. Sprinkle with the parsley.

Serve with rice or noodles.

CHICKEN AND RICE

⅓ cup shortening
3 onions, chopped
2 3-pound chickens, disjointed
2 teaspoons salt
¼ teaspoon freshly ground black
  pepper
⅛ teaspoon saffron
1 cup rice
3 cups chicken stock or canned
  consommé
2 tomatoes, peeled and chopped
1 bay leaf
2 green peppers, sliced

Melt the shortening in a saucepan. Add the onions and chicken. Cook over medium heat until browned. Add the salt, pepper, saffron, and rice. Cook for 5 minutes, stirring constantly. Add the stock, tomatoes, bay leaf, and green peppers.

Cover and cook over low heat for 30 minutes, or until chicken and rice are tender. Add a little boiling water while cooking if necessary. Discard bay leaf, and correct seasoning.

When ready, the rice should be fairly moist, but there should be no liquid remaining.

This recipe is My Sammy's favorite. He says he likes soup with lots of things in it and this Chicken in the Pot satisfies his, he calls it, his taste buds. I say it's chicken with a little soup and Sammy says it's soup with a lot of chicken. So who wants to argue as long as he eats it? Whatever is your thoughts about this, rest assured it tastes very good and the kneidlach *wouldn't disappoint you neither. My Sammy, who knows about these things, said once upon a time a king thought it was pretty good too. King Henry (maybe it was the fourth one) once said that he wished everybody in his kingdom would have a chicken in his pot on Sunday. Personally, I like it better on Friday night.*

CHICKEN IN THE POT WITH KNEIDLACH SAMUEL GOLDBERG (DUMPLINGS)

1 5-pound chicken (soup chicken), disjointed
Feet, neck, and giblets of chicken
10 cups water
1 onion
2 stalks celery
2 carrots
1 parsnip
4 sprigs parsley
1 tablespoon salt

Place the chicken, feet, neck, giblets, and water in a saucepan. Bring to a boil. Skim the top. Cover and cook over medium heat for 1 hour. Add the onion, celery, carrots, parsnip, parsley, and salt. Cook for 1 hour additional, or until the chicken is tender. Strain the soup into a separate saucepan. Now prepare the *kneidlach* (dumplings):

2 egg yolks
½ teaspoon salt
2 tablespoons melted shortening
½ cup matzo meal
2 egg whites, stiffly beaten

Beat the egg yolks, salt, and shortening together. Add the matzo meal and mix well. Fold in the egg whites thoroughly. Chill for 10 minutes. Form into 2-inch balls. Drop into the boiling soup. Cover and cook for 20 minutes.

Serve the soup with the dumplings and pieces of the chicken. This dish constitutes a complete meal in one dish.

I put this recipe down in honor of Uncle David, but it's not only for him. I make it for Uncle David and all his friends whenever they come for supper. So why should this be a special recipe for only them? I'll tell you. It's simple. Uncle David is already in his late sixties (this is by his figures, by mine I can't tell you because he wouldn't like it). His friends are already in the same category and between all of them there isn't an original tooth, so the Fricassee of Chicken is very soft and succulent and very easy to take. If you have an Uncle David by you, you might try this, but it isn't necessary. If you are in charge of all your faculties it's also enjoyable.

CHICKEN FRICASSEE
À LA UNCLE DAVID

2 teaspoons salt
½ teaspoon freshly ground black pepper
2 teaspoons paprika
2 cloves garlic
2 4-pound chickens, disjointed
4 tablespoons shortening
3 onions, chopped
½ cup boiling water

Mix the salt, pepper, paprika, and garlic to a paste. Rub into the chicken very well.

Heat the shortening in a heavy skillet or a Dutch oven. Brown the chicken in it. Add the onions and cook over medium heat until the onions are brown, stirring occasionally. Add the water. Cover and cook over low heat for 2 hours, or until the chicken is tender.

Serve with boiled rice, dumplings, or *nockerl*.

GOLDEN CHICKEN

> 6 dried mushrooms
> 1 7-pound chicken (pullet), disjointed
> 4 cups boiling water
> 1 tablespoon salt
> ½ teaspoon freshly ground black pepper
> 2 tablespoons rendered chicken fat
> 1 tablespoon flour
> 1-inch piece lemon rind
> 3 egg yolks

Soak the mushrooms in water to cover for 15 minutes. Drain.

Combine the chicken, boiling water, salt, pepper, and mushrooms in a saucepan. Bring to a boil. Cover and cook over medium heat for 2¼ hours, or until chicken is tender. Remove the chicken and keep warm. Strain 1½ cups of the stock and reserve.

Heat the chicken fat in a saucepan. Add the flour, stirring until smooth. Add the strained stock, stirring constantly until the boiling point. Add the lemon rind and cook over low heat for 5 minutes. Discard lemon rind.

Beat the egg yolks in a bowl. Gradually add the previous sauce, stirring constantly to prevent curdling. Return the mixture to the saucepan. Reheat, but do not allow to boil.

Pour over the chicken and serve.

ROAST CAPON WITH BARLEY STUFFING

¾ cup pearl barley
3 teaspoons salt
¾ teaspoon freshly ground black pepper
1 teaspoon paprika
2 cloves garlic, minced
1 7-pound capon
3 tablespoons shortening
2 onions, chopped
1 carrot, sliced
2 stalks celery, sliced
3 sprigs parsley, chopped
6 slices white bread, toasted and cut into cubes

Soak the barley in water to cover for 2 hours. Drain. Add fresh water and cook for 1½ hours. Drain well.

Mix 1½ teaspoons of the salt, ½ teaspoon of the pepper, the paprika, and garlic together. Rub into the capon.

Melt the shortening in a skillet. Add the onions, carrot, celery, and parsley. Sauté for 10 minutes, stirring frequently. Add the bread, barley, and remaining salt and pepper. Mix together. Stuff the capon with the mixture, closing the opening with thread, skewers, or aluminum foil. Place in a roasting pan.

Roast in a 350° oven for 2½ hours, or until browned and tender.

Meats

If you have a good butcher like my Hazelkorn, the butcher, you have good meat, especially if you are in the store and can see what he cuts for you. What you do with the meat when you get it home is another question. In my house I have to have meat. Mr. Goldberg, My Husband, thinks it's not a meal without some kind of meat, and no matter what kind of a meal I serve there's always meat for My Jake (Mr. Goldberg). With two men in the house it's very difficult sometimes because by Jake any meat is good, but with Sammy (My Son) it's not meat unless it's steak. So what do I do? I cook my meat as tasty as possible, and when Sammy enters the house the aroma of the fumes of the meat makes him hungry. The result? He eats whichsoever I set down on the table.

ROAST BEEF

2 tablespoons flour
2 cloves garlic, minced
½ teaspoon freshly ground black
   pepper
8-pound rib roast, or 4 pounds
   rolled roast
3 onions, sliced
3 tomatoes, chopped
1 cup boiling water
3 green peppers, quartered
4 potatoes, peeled and quartered
2 teaspoons salt

Mix the flour, garlic, and pepper together. Rub into the roast. Place in a roasting pan. Roast in a 350° oven for 30 minutes. Pour off the fat.

Add the onions and tomatoes, and roast for 20 minutes. Add the water. Continue roasting to desired degree of rareness, adding the peppers, potatoes, and salt 30 minutes before the meat is ready. Baste occasionally.

For rare meat, roast for a total of 20 minutes per pound, 25 minutes a pound for medium, and 35 minutes a pound for well done.

ROAST BEEF WITH VEGETABLES

1 tablespoon salt
¾ teaspoon pepper
2 cloves garlic, minced
4 pounds beef (brisket, eye
  round, or similar cut)
4 onions, sliced
4 carrots, scraped and quartered
2 tomatoes, quartered
2 bay leaves
3 potatoes, peeled and quartered

Mix the salt, pepper, and garlic to a paste; rub into the meat. Place in a roasting pan. Arrange the onions, carrots, tomatoes, and bay leaves around it. Roast in a 350° oven 2½ hours, adding boiling water if pan becomes dry. Add the potatoes; roast 45 minutes longer, or until meat and potatoes are tender.

Place the meat and potatoes on a platter. Force the gravy through a sieve and serve separately.

BOILED BEEF

2 quarts water
2 onions
2 carrots
1 celery root
1 parsnip
4 pounds beef (brisket or plate
  flank)
1 bay leaf
1 tablespoon salt
¼ teaspoon freshly ground black
  pepper

Combine the water, onions, carrots, celery root, and parsnip in a saucepan. Bring to a boil and add the beef and bay leaf. Cover and cook over low heat for 2½ hours. Add the salt and pepper. Cook 15 minutes longer, or until the meat is tender. Discard the bay leaf.

Serve the soup with noodles or matzo balls. Serve the meat separately with horseradish.

Pot Roast is all kinds of things to all kinds of people. To me it's a compliment, and if I do say so myself, I make it out of this world. It's not only my opinion but the opinion of my severest critic and biggest eater, Sammy. He says it's not Pot Roast, it's nostalgia, and no matter where he is he would be able to smell it cooking even a thousand miles away. That's a lovely compliment and a wonderful recommendation. Try it.

GEDEMPTE FLEISCH

POT ROAST OF BEEF
HOME STYLE

2 teaspoons salt
½ teaspoon freshly ground black pepper
1 teaspoon paprika
4 pounds beef (brisket, eye round, or cross rib)
4 onions, chopped
2 cloves garlic, minced

Combine the salt, pepper, and paprika. Rub into the beef thoroughly. Heat a Dutch oven or heavy saucepan. Place the meat in it and brown well over medium heat on all sides. Add the onions and garlic.

Continue browning over medium heat for 10 minutes. Cover and cook over low heat for 2½ hours, or until the meat is tender. Turn the meat frequently. Add a little water if necessary.

Slice, and serve with the gravy. Serve with potato pancakes.

BEEF AND KASHA (BUCKWHEAT GROATS)

> 1 cup small dried lima beans
> 3 pounds beef (brisket or chuck roast)
> 2 onions, chopped
> 1 clove garlic, minced
> 2½ teaspoons salt
> ½ teaspoon freshly ground black pepper
> 1 teaspoon paprika
> 1 cup buckwheat groats (*kasha*)
> 4 cups boiling water

Wash the beans well. Cover with water in a saucepan. Bring to a boil; remove from the heat and let soak for 1 hour. Drain.

Place the meat, onions, and garlic in a Dutch oven or heavy saucepan. Cook over medium heat until browned. Sprinkle with the salt, pepper, and paprika. Add the beans, buckwheat groats, and water. Cover and cook over low heat for 2½ hours, or until meat and beans are tender. Add a little more boiling water if necessary.

ESSIG FLEISCH

SWEET AND SOUR MEAT

4 pounds beef (brisket, short
ribs, or plate flank)
5 onions, chopped
2 teaspoons salt
1½ cups boiling water
3 tablespoons sugar
4 tablespoons lemon juice

Heat a heavy skillet or Dutch oven. Add the beef. Brown well on all sides. Add the onions; cook over low heat until onions are brown, stirring frequently. Add the salt and boiling water. Cover and cook over low heat for 2 hours. Add the sugar and lemon juice. Cook for 30 minutes longer, or until the meat is tender. Correct seasoning. Add more sugar or lemon juice to taste, bearing in mind that the dish should have both a sweet and a sour taste. Slice the meat, and return to the gravy for 30 minutes, removing the skillet from the heat.

Heat for 15 minutes before serving. Boiled potatoes or noodles may be served with this dish.

BEEF AND SAUERKRAUT

2 teaspoons salt
½ teaspoon freshly ground black
pepper
1 teaspoon paprika
4 pounds brisket, cross rib, or
chuck roast of beef
2 onions, chopped
2 pounds sauerkraut, drained
1 teaspoon caraway seeds

Combine the salt, pepper, and paprika. Sprinkle on the beef, and pound or rub it in well. Heat a Dutch oven or heavy saucepan and place the meat in it. Cook over high heat until brown on all sides.

97

Add the onions and continue browning. Cover and cook over low heat for ½ hour. Add the sauerkraut and caraway seeds and cook for an additional 2 hours, or until tender. Baste and turn the meat frequently, adding a little water if necessary.

Slice the meat and serve with the sauerkraut. This dish is often served with mashed potatoes.

MEAT-STUFFED PRUNES

24 large unsweetened prunes
6 tablespoons shortening
1 onion, chopped
½ pound ground beef
½ cup crushed canned
    pineapple, drained
4 tablespoons lemon juice
3 tablespoons brown sugar
3 onions, sliced thin
1 cup canned tomato sauce
4 gingersnaps, crushed
1½ teaspoons salt
¼ teaspoon freshly ground black
    pepper

Soak the prunes overnight in water to cover. (This step may be omitted if the presoaked variety is used.) Drain. Pit very carefully.

Melt 2 tablespoons of the shortening in a skillet. Add the chopped onion and sauté for 5 minutes, stirring frequently. Add the beef, pineapple, 1 tablespoon of the lemon juice, and 1 tablespoon of the brown sugar. Cook over low heat for 10 minutes, stirring frequently. Stuff the prunes with the mixture.

Melt the remaining shortening in a saucepan. Sauté the sliced onions in it for 10 minutes, stirring frequently. Add the tomato sauce, gingersnaps, salt, pepper, and remaining lemon juice and sugar. Add the prunes carefully, open side up. Cover and cook over low heat for 25 minutes. Correct seasoning. The sauce should be both sweet and sour.

Serve as an accompaniment to meat or poultry dishes, or as a main course with potatoes.

ROLLED MEAT LOAF

> 1 cup medium buckwheat groats (*kasha*)
> 2 cups boiling water
> 3 tablespoons salt
> 4 tablespoons shortening
> 3 pounds ground beef
> 2 egg yolks
> 1 onion, grated
> ¼ cup bread crumbs
> ½ teaspoon freshly ground black pepper
> 2 tablespoons flour

Combine the buckwheat groats, boiling water, 1 teaspoon of the salt, and 2 tablespoons of the shortening in the top of a double boiler. Place over boiling water and cook over medium heat for 25 minutes, or until the groats are dry.

Mix the beef with the egg yolks, onion, bread crumbs, pepper, and remaining salt. Mix well. Pat the meat into a square 1 inch thick on a lightly floured surface. Place the groats on top and roll up carefully.

Heat the remaining shortening in a baking dish. Place the roll in it carefully.

Bake in a 400° oven for 45 minutes.

When I was a young bride and this was the first time my mother-in-law was coming to my house for supper I didn't know how to cook her. How should I make a good impression? First, what I cooked had to be good; second, it shouldn't be extravagant—so what should I make? For my mother-in-law supper without soup was no supper, and that remained with My Jake also. If my butcher would give me a bone, I would make barley soup, and if I bought a pound of soup meat, I could use it in the soup and then make Meat and Sauerkraut. The menu was:

> Barley Soup
> Meat and Sauerkraut
> Apple Compote
> Tea and Spongecake

After that supper I was her favorite daughter-in-law.

LEFTOVER MEAT AND SAUERKRAUT

2 pounds sauerkraut
3 tablespoons shortening
2 onions, chopped
¼ pound mushrooms, sliced
6 slices cooked beef, veal,
    chicken, or turkey
12 ripe olives, sliced
2 dill pickles, sliced

Wash the sauerkraut. Cover with water in a saucepan. Bring to a boil and cook for 15 minutes. Drain well.

Melt the shortening in a skillet. Sauté the onions in it for 10 minutes, stirring frequently. Add the sauerkraut and mushrooms. Cook over medium heat for 10 minutes, stirring frequently.

Place half of the sauerkraut in a greased baking dish. Arrange the meat over it. Spread half of the olives and pickles over it. Cover with the remaining sauerkraut, olives, and pickles.

Bake in a 375° oven for 20 minutes.

MEAT AND CARROT TZIMMES

3 teaspoons salt
½ teaspoon freshly ground black pepper
3 pounds beef (brisket or chuck)
2 onions, chopped
2 tablespoons flour
3 cups boiling water
4 tablespoons honey
8 carrots, quartered
2 sweet potatoes, peeled and quartered

Mix together 2 teaspoons of the salt and the pepper. Rub into the beef thoroughly.

Place the meat in a casserole or Dutch oven with the onions. Brown slowly over low heat. Add the flour, mixing well. Add the water, stirring until the boiling point. Cover and cook over low heat for 1 hour. Add the honey and mix. Add the carrots, sweet potatoes, and remaining salt. Cover.

Bake in a 375° oven for 1½ hours, or until beef is tender. Remove the cover for the last 15 minutes of baking. Correct seasoning.

RUMANIAN MEAT AND PEPPERS

3 tablespoons shortening
1½ pounds beef, cubed
1½ pounds veal, cubed
4 onions, chopped
2 teaspoons salt
½ teaspoon freshly ground black
  pepper
½ cup boiling water
6 green peppers, sliced thin
4 tomatoes, peeled and sliced
2 cloves garlic, minced
3 tablespoons chopped parsley

Melt the shortening in a heavy saucepan. Add the beef, veal, and onions. Cook over medium heat until browned. Add the salt, pepper, and water. Cover and cook over low heat for 1½ hours. Add the green peppers, tomatoes, garlic, and parsley. Re-cover the saucepan.

Bake in a 375° oven for 15 minutes. Remove the cover and bake for 15 minutes additional.

KOKLETIN

SPICY HAMBURGERS

2 pounds ground beef
1 onion, grated
2 cloves garlic, minced
2 eggs, beaten
¼ cup cold water
3 tablespoons bread crumbs
2 teaspoons salt
½ teaspoon freshly ground black
  pepper
4 tablespoons shortening

Mix the beef, onion, garlic, eggs, water, bread crumbs, salt, and pepper together until well blended. Shape into 12 croquettes.

Melt the shortening in a skillet. Fry the croquettes in it for 10 minutes on each side. (*Kokletin* are not eaten rare.)

Serve with home-fried potatoes.

MEAT BALLS IN MUSHROOM SAUCE

> 1½ pounds ground beef
> 1 onion, grated
> 2 teaspoons salt
> ¼ teaspoon pepper
> 3 tablespoons cold water
> 1 egg
> 3 tablespoons bread crumbs
> 4 tablespoons shortening
> 1 pound mushrooms, sliced
> 2 egg yolks
> 2 tablespoons lemon juice
> 2 tablespoons chopped parsley

Mix the beef, onion, salt, pepper, water, egg, and bread crumbs until smooth. Shape into 1-inch balls. Melt 2 tablespoons shortening in a skillet and fry the balls in it to desired degree of rareness.

Melt remaining shortening in a skillet. Sauté the mushrooms in it for 10 minutes. Beat the egg yolks and lemon juice together and add to the mushrooms, stirring constantly to prevent curdling. Add the meat balls. Cook over low heat for 5 minutes, but do not allow to boil.

Sprinkle the parsley on top and serve.

POT ROAST WITH APRICOTS

1 pound dried apricots
2 tablespoons shortening
4 pounds beef (brisket or chuck
    roast)
3 cups boiling water
1 onion, grated
2 teaspoons salt
¼ teaspoon freshly ground black
    pepper
2 teaspoons lemon juice
1 teaspoon sugar

Soak the apricots overnight in water to cover. Drain.

Melt the shortening in a heavy saucepan or Dutch oven. Brown the meat in it over medium heat; turn meat frequently. Add the boiling water, onion, salt, pepper, lemon juice, sugar, and apricots. Cover and cook over low heat for 2½ hours, or until meat is tender. Add a little water if necessary. Correct seasoning.

BEEF AND LENTIL STEW

1 cup lentils
2 tablespoons shortening
2 onions, chopped
2 pounds boneless beef, cubed
2 cups boiling water
2 teaspoons salt
½ teaspoon freshly ground black
    pepper
1 teaspoon paprika
¼ cup rice

Wash the lentils thoroughly, discarding any imperfect ones. Soak in water to cover for 2 hours (if the presoaked variety is not used). Drain.

Melt the shortening in a saucepan. Add the onions and beef. Cook over medium heat for 15 minutes, stirring frequently. Add the lentils, water, salt, pepper, and paprika. Cover and cook over low heat for 1½ hours. Add the rice, and a little more water if necessary.

Cook for 20 minutes longer, or until rice and lentils are tender.

MAMALIGA PIE

CORN MEAL AND MEAT PIE

1 cup yellow corn meal
1 cup cold water
4 cups boiling water
2 teaspoons salt
3 tablespoons shortening
1 onion, chopped
1 green pepper, chopped
1 clove garlic, minced
1 pound chopped beef
1 egg, beaten
¼ cup bread crumbs
½ teaspoon pepper

Mix the corn meal and cold water to a smooth paste. Add to the boiling water, stirring constantly. Add 1 teaspoon salt. Cook over low heat for 10 minutes, stirring occasionally.

Heat the shortening in a skillet. Sauté the onion, green pepper, and garlic in it for 10 minutes. Add to the beef. Mix well. Add the egg, bread crumbs, pepper, and remaining salt. Mix well.

Spread half the corn meal on the bottom of a 9-inch greased pie plate. Arrange the meat mixture over it and cover with the remaining corn meal. Grease a piece of aluminum foil and cover the top of the pie plate with it.

Bake in a 350° oven for 1 hour. Cut into pie-shaped wedges and serve hot.

This is a dish that you can't spoil. Some things that you can cook have to be eaten right away, but with this recipe you can cook it forever or until you're ready to eat it. I know that when I am going to have certain individuals for dinner, who will be nameless because they would be insulted, I will not be able to eat on time. I don't know the reason, but they scraggle in one at a time and a 7 o'clock supper becomes an 8 P.M. dinner. Punctuality is not one of their faults. So if you happen to have the same trouble you can be sure that this recipe will serve you very well. Also, you can eat on time with this dish. Either way, you will find it's a pleasure.

BEEF WITH PRUNES AND SWEET POTATOES

2 teaspoons salt
½ teaspoon freshly ground black pepper
3 pounds beef (brisket, cross rib, or chuck roast)
1 pound unsweetened prunes, presoaked
3 cups water
3 sweet potatoes, peeled and quartered
2 tablespoons lemon juice
3 tablespoons brown sugar

Sprinkle the salt and pepper on the beef and rub in thoroughly.

Brown the meat on all sides in a Dutch oven or heavy saucepan. Cover and cook over low heat for 1 hour, turning the meat frequently. Add the prunes, water, sweet potatoes, lemon juice, and sugar. Cover and cook over low heat for 1½ hours additional.

Uncover and place in a 350° oven for 30 minutes, or until the beef is tender.

STUFFED BREAST OF VEAL

4 teaspoons salt
1 teaspoon freshly ground black pepper
2 teaspoons paprika
2 cloves garlic, minced
Breast of veal, with pocket for stuffing
4 potatoes, peeled, grated, and drained
1 onion, grated
1 egg, beaten
½ cup flour
½ cup melted shortening
2 onions, chopped
½ cup boiling water

Combine 2½ teaspoons of the salt, ¾ teaspoon of the pepper, the paprika, and garlic. Rub into the veal thoroughly.

Mix the potatoes, grated onion, egg, flour, ¼ cup of the shortening, and remaining salt and pepper until very smooth. Stuff the mixture into the pocket of the veal, fastening the opening with skewers or toothpicks. Place in a roasting pan. Add the chopped onions and remaining shortening.

Roast in a 400° oven for 25 minutes. Reduce heat to 325° and add the boiling water. Roast for an additional 2½ hours, or until the veal is tender. Baste frequently, adding a little more water if necessary.

POTTED VEAL WITH
FARFEL (EGG BARLEY)

6 tablespoons shortening
4 onions, sliced thin
2 tablespoons paprika
3 pounds boneless veal, cubed
2 teaspoons salt
¼ teaspoon freshly ground black
   pepper
1 teaspoon caraway seeds
1 cup boiling water
3 cups cooked *farfel* (egg barley)

Melt half the shortening in a saucepan. Add the onions. Sauté for 10 minutes, stirring frequently. Add the paprika, and mix. Add the veal. Brown on all sides. Add the salt, pepper, caraway seeds, and water. Cover and cook over low heat for 1½ hours. Correct seasoning.

Melt the remaining shortening in a skillet. Add the *farfel*; fry until lightly browned.

Serve the veal with the *farfel* around it.

BAKED VEAL CHOPS

2 teaspoons salt
½ teaspoon freshly ground black
   pepper
6 veal chops, ¾ inch thick
1 cup matzo or cracker meal
2 eggs
6 tablespoons shortening
3 onions, sliced ½ inch thick

Mix 1 teaspoon of the salt and ¼ teaspoon of the pepper together. Sprinkle on the chops. Dip the chops in the matzo meal, coating them well. Beat the eggs with the remaining salt and pepper. Dip the chops in the eggs.

Heat 4 tablespoons of the shortening in a skillet. Brown the chops on both sides. Place in a greased baking dish.

Heat the remaining shortening in the same skillet. Sauté the onions in it for 10 minutes, stirring frequently. Place the onions over the chops.

Bake in a 325° oven for 45 minutes.

HUNGARIAN BREAST OF VEAL

> 3 teaspoons salt
> ¾ teaspoon freshly ground black pepper
> 2 teaspoons paprika
> Breast of veal, with pocket for stuffing
> ½ cup boiling water
> 2 slices white bread, untrimmed
> 4 tablespoons shortening
> 4 onions, chopped
> ¼ pound mushrooms, sliced
> 1 cup cooked green peas
> 1 egg
> 1 egg yolk
> 1 cup canned tomato sauce

Combine half of the salt, pepper, and paprika. Rub into the veal thoroughly.

Pour the boiling water over the bread. Soak for 2 minutes. Squeeze out excess water.

Melt the shortening in a skillet. Add half the onions. Sauté for 10 minutes. Add the mushrooms and sauté for 5 minutes. Add the green peas and bread. Sauté for 2 minutes, stirring constantly. Remove from the heat. Add the egg, egg yolk, and remaining salt, pepper, and paprika. Mix well. Stuff the veal with the mixture. Close the opening with skewers or with thread. Place in a roasting pan and add the remaining onions.

Roast in a 400° oven for 30 minutes. Reduce heat to 350°. Add the tomato sauce and continue roasting for 2½ hours longer, or until veal is tender. Baste frequently, adding a little water if necessary.

One of Solly's patients was a cook in a very fancy restaurant and as a favor to Solly he gave him this recipe. What they call it in the restaurant I don't know, but by us we call it after Solly because it's the one thing he can cook and because David wouldn't be happy unless his son's name was in the book too.

SOLLY "THE DOCTOR'S" VEAL CROQUETTES

½ cup shortening
2 onions, chopped
5 slices white bread, trimmed
¾ cup boiling water
2 pounds ground veal
2 teaspoons salt
½ teaspoon freshly ground black pepper
4 eggs
3 tablespoons cold water
1 cup bread crumbs

Melt 2 tablespoons of the shortening in a skillet. Sauté the onions in it for 10 minutes, stirring frequently. Soak the bread in the water for 5 minutes. Drain and mash. Mix the veal, salt, pepper, 2 of the eggs, the cold water, and onions together until smooth. Shape the mixture into 12 oblong croquettes.

Beat the remaining eggs. Dip the croquettes in the eggs and then in the bread crumbs, coating them well.

Melt half of the remaining shortening in a skillet. Fry the croquettes in it over low heat until well browned, about 10 minutes on each side. Add more shortening as required.

GEDEMPTE VEAL CHOPS

BRAISED VEAL CHOPS

2 cloves garlic, minced
2 teaspoons salt
½ teaspoon freshly ground black pepper
1½ teaspoons paprika
6 veal chops, ¾ inch thick
6 tablespoons shortening
3 onions, chopped
4 tablespoons water
3 potatoes, half cooked, drained, and sliced

Make a paste of the garlic, salt, pepper, and paprika. Rub it into the chops.

Melt the shortening in a skillet. Brown the chops and onions in it over low heat. Add the water. Cover and cook over low heat for 30 minutes. Add the potatoes. Cover and cook for 15 minutes, or until the chops are tender. Stir frequently. Add a little additional water if necessary.

VEAL PAPRIKAS

3 tablespoons shortening
3 onions, chopped
1 clove garlic, minced
3 pounds veal, cut into 2-inch
  cubes
2 green peppers, diced
2 teaspoons salt
¼ teaspoon freshly ground black
  pepper
1 tablespoon paprika
3 tomatoes, chopped
3 potatoes, peeled and cubed

Melt the shortening in a Dutch oven or a heavy saucepan. Add the onions, garlic, and veal. Cover and cook over medium heat until the meat browns, stirring frequently. Add the green peppers, salt, pepper, paprika, and tomatoes.

Cover and cook over low heat for 1½ hours. Stir frequently and add a little water if necessary. Add the potatoes and cook for 25 minutes additional. Correct seasoning.

SALAMI AND EGGS

12 slices salami
6 eggs, beaten
2 tablespoons water
¼ teaspoon pepper

Fry the salami in a skillet for 2 minutes on each side. (If the skillet is not large enough to hold all the salami flat, use 2 skillets.)

Mix the eggs, water, and pepper together. Pour over the salami. Cook over low heat until the eggs are set, lifting the edges to allow the egg to run under.

Serve as a large pancake.

Moyshe can't cook, so he didn't make up this recipe. I named it after him because he's a learned man. One day we were all eating and David and his friend Moyshe were talking. Moyshe remarked how sometimes people take for granted the things around them, for instance the Chulent we were eating. What does the name mean Moyshe asked, and who could answer? It's German, he said. It means Schul ent in German—the end of synagogue services—and Chulent was eaten after the services because it could be made the day before and reheated after synagogue. An easy dish to make, certainly, but the knowledge to know what it means, that doesn't come so easy.

CHULENT MOYSHE

LIMA BEANS AND MEAT
CASSEROLE

1 cup dried lima beans
3 tablespoons rendered chicken
   fat or salad oil
3 onions, chopped
4 potatoes, peeled and quartered
½ cup barley
3 pounds short ribs of beef
1 tablespoon salt
1 teaspoon freshly ground black
   pepper
1 teaspoon paprika
1 tablespoon flour

Wash the beans thoroughly. Soak them in hot water to cover for 2 hours. Drain.

Heat the chicken fat in a heavy saucepan. Add the onions and sauté for 10 minutes, stirring frequently. Add the beans, potatoes, and barley, and stir. Place the meat in the center of the pot. Combine the salt, pepper, paprika, and flour, and sprinkle on top. Add boiling water to cover ½ inch above the top of the ingredients.

Cover and cook over very low heat for 5 hours. Check the pot frequently to see that it does not burn, adding a little water if necessary. If desired, the *chulent* may be baked in a 325° oven for the same length of time; check the dish frequently. The finished *chulent* should be quite thick, with practically no liquid remaining.

SWEET AND SOUR TONGUE

> 1 pickled tongue (about 4–5 pounds)
> 2 tablespoons shortening
> 1 onion, chopped
> ½ cup brown sugar
> ½ teaspoon salt
> ¼ cup cider vinegar
> 4 gingersnaps, crushed
> ¼ cup seedless raisins
> ¼ cup blanched almonds
> 1 lemon, sliced very thin

Wash the tongue well. Place in a deep saucepan with water to cover. Bring to a boil and cover the saucepan. Cook over medium heat for 3 hours, or until tender. (Taste the water; if too salty, change the water, replacing with boiling water.) Plunge the tongue into cold water. Drain and trim. Reserve 1¼ cups of the stock.

Melt the shortening in a saucepan. Add the onion and sauté for 5 minutes, stirring frequently. Add the sugar, salt, vinegar, and stock. Cook over low heat for 5 minutes. Add the gingersnaps, stirring until dissolved. Add the raisins, almonds, and lemon. Cook over low heat for 10 minutes.

Slice the tongue and serve with the sauce.

114

My family loves a picnic, like on July the IV, and they are so impatient to eat I don't know why we even bother to go. If you think they go on a picnic to look at nature you're very wrong. They go to eat. For each and every picnic I make Baked Tongue, never by request, only as an order from one and all, and by the time we get to where we want to picnic there isn't a snitch left. No matter how well I wrap the tongue and no matter where I store the picnic basket, the aroma must leak through. It doesn't take ten minutes of riding in the car before someone says, "Let's sample the tongue." Only it's not just a sample, it's the whole output, but it's my pleasure and don't you think they know it?

BAKED TONGUE

1 fresh tongue (4–6 pounds)
2 onions, sliced
2 cloves garlic, minced
2 teaspoons salt
½ teaspoon freshly ground black
  pepper
1 bay leaf
3 tomatoes, chopped
2 cups stock, or 1 can consommé
  and ½ cup water
4 potatoes, peeled and quartered

Place the tongue in a bowl. Pour boiling water over it and allow to soak for 10 minutes. Trim and peel the tongue.

Place the tongue in a roasting pan. Add the onions, garlic, salt, pepper, bay leaf, tomatoes, and stock. Cover the pan.

Roast in a 325° oven for 2½ hours, basting frequently. Add the potatoes and continue roasting uncovered for 45 minutes, or until the tongue and potatoes are tender. This dish is often served with spinach.

LIVER AND DUMPLINGS

1½ cups sifted flour
3 teaspoons salt
1 egg
½ cup cold water
3 tablespoons shortening
2 onions, sliced
6 slices calf's liver
¼ teaspoon freshly ground black pepper
¼ teaspoon paprika
2 tablespoons potato flour
1½ cups boiling water

Sift the flour and 1 teaspoon of the salt into a bowl. Beat the egg and water together and add, beating until smooth. Drop by the teaspoonful into rapidly boiling salted water. Cook until they rise to the surface, about 6 minutes. Drain and keep warm.

Melt the shortening in a skillet. Add the onions; sauté for 5 minutes, stirring frequently. Add the liver and sauté until brown. Sprinkle with the pepper, paprika, and remaining salt. Remove the liver to a platter and keep warm. Sprinkle the potato flour on the onions remaining in the skillet, mixing until smooth. Add the boiling water, stirring constantly until the boiling point. Cook over low heat for 3 minutes.

Place the dumplings around the liver and pour the gravy over all.

This recipe got its name from My Rich Cousin Simon. You would think that a man as well-to-do as My Rich Cousin Simon would have a fancier dish named after him, but not so. This is Simon's favorite dish because this is what my mother made for supper when Simon dropped in and met his future wife-to-be. She's not so future any more because they've been married twenty years already. Not a sentimental man, My Cousin Simon, but in some things he's a poet, so we named this goulash after him.

FRANKFURTER GOULASH COUSIN SIMON

2 tablespoons shortening
4 onions, chopped
1 clove garlic, minced
3 green peppers, diced
1 can (#2½) tomatoes
1 teaspoon salt
½ teaspoon freshly ground black pepper
12 beef frankfurters, cut into 2-inch pieces

Melt the shortening in a saucepan. Add the onions and garlic. Sauté for 10 minutes, stirring frequently. Add the green peppers and sauté for 5 minutes. Add the tomatoes, salt, and pepper, and mix well. Cook over low heat for 1 hour. Add the frankfurters. Cook over low heat for 30 minutes. Correct seasoning.

Serve with noodles or boiled potatoes.

FRANKFURTERS WITH SAUERKRAUT

2 tablespoons shortening
1 pound sauerkraut, drained
2 onions, sliced thin
2 cups water
1 potato, peeled and grated
1 teaspoon sugar
1 teaspoon salt
¼ teaspoon freshly ground black
  pepper
1 teaspoon caraway seeds
  (optional)
6 to 12 beef frankfurters

Melt the shortening in a saucepan. Add the sauerkraut and onions.
Cook over high heat for 5 minutes, stirring almost constantly. Add
the water. Cover and cook over low heat for 1½ hours. Add the
potato, sugar, salt, pepper, and caraway seeds. Cover and cook for 30
minutes longer.

Cook the frankfurters in boiling water for 5 minutes. Drain and
add to the sauerkraut. Cook for 10 minutes.

FRANKFURTERS AND PEPPERS

2 tablespoons shortening
4 onions, sliced
9 frankfurters, cut into 2-inch
  pieces
2 tablespoons chopped parsley
4 green peppers, cut into ½-inch
  slices
4 tomatoes, sliced
1 teaspoon salt
¼ teaspoon freshly ground black
  pepper

Melt the shortening in a deep skillet. Add the onions. Sauté for 10 minutes, stirring frequently. Add the frankfurters. Cook over medium heat for 5 minutes, stirring frequently. Add the parsley, green peppers, tomatoes, salt, and pepper. Mix lightly. Cook over low heat for 15 minutes, or until peppers are tender. Correct seasoning and serve.

SWEETBREADS AND MUSHROOMS

> 3 pairs sweetbreads
> 1 tablespoon vinegar
> 2 teaspoons salt
> 3 tablespoons shortening
> 2 onions, chopped
> ½ pound mushrooms, sliced
> 2 tablespoons flour
> ¼ teaspoon freshly ground black pepper
> 1 cup cooked or canned green peas
> 2 tablespoons chopped parsley

Wash the sweetbreads. Place in a saucepan with the vinegar, salt, and cold water to cover. Bring to a boil. Cover and cook over medium heat for 20 minutes. Drain, reserving 1 cup of the stock. Cover the sweetbreads with cold water for 30 minutes. Drain; remove the membrane and cut the sweetbreads into cubes.

Melt the shortening in a skillet. Add the onions. Sauté for 10 minutes, stirring frequently. Add the mushrooms and sauté for 10 minutes additional. Sprinkle with the flour, mixing steadily. Add the reserved stock, stirring constantly until the boiling point. Add the pepper, peas, parsley, and sweetbreads. Cover and cook over low heat for 10 minutes. Correct seasoning.

Serve in patty shells.

My neighbor Mrs. Cawley makes Corned Beef like nobody. It is without a doubt and without the slightest question of a shadow the best. When I asked her for the recipe she told me this story. When she first got married her husband expressed a desire for Corned Beef and cabbage. The cabbage she knew about, the Corned Beef was beyond her vocabulary at the moment. So she went to her butcher and asked him how she should make it. He didn't know but he got the recipe from his wife, and Mrs. Cawley tried it. Mr. Cawley said it was the best he ever ate, but she wasn't sure whether it was love or the truth. They've been married now for twelve (12) years and Mr. Cawley hasn't lost his taste for Corned Beef, so it must have been the truth. What could be a better recommendation?

MRS. CAWLEY'S CORNED BEEF

1½ cups salt
4 quarts water
1 tablespoon sugar
2 tablespoons pickling spice
½ ounce saltpeter
8 bay leaves
5-pound brisket of beef
8 cloves garlic

Combine the salt, water, sugar, pickling spice, saltpeter, and bay leaves in a saucepan. Boil for 5 minutes. Cool.

Place the beef and garlic in a stone crock or glass container. Pour the spice mixture over it. Place a weight on the meat to keep it submerged. Place a piece of cheesecloth or muslin across the top of the container and tie it in place. Place the cover of the container on top. Allow to pickle for 12 days in a cool place.

Remove the beef and rinse. Place in a saucepan with water to cover. Bring to a boil and skim the top. Cook for 3 hours, or until the corned beef is tender.

Tongue may be pickled in the same way.

LAMB GOULASH

> 2 teaspoons salt
> ½ teaspoon freshly ground black pepper
> 2 teaspoons paprika
> 2 cloves garlic, minced
> 3 pounds lamb, cubed
> 3 tablespoons shortening
> 2 onions, chopped
> 2 green peppers, diced
> 1 cup canned tomato sauce
> 2 potatoes, peeled and cubed
> ¼ pound string beans, cut in half
> ½ pound green peas, shelled
> 2 carrots, sliced

Mix the salt, pepper, paprika, and garlic to a smooth paste. Lightly roll the lamb in it.

Melt the shortening in a Dutch oven or a heavy skillet. Add the lamb and onions. Cook over medium heat until browned, stirring occasionally. Add the green peppers and tomato sauce. Cover and cook over low heat for 1½ hours. Add the potatoes, string beans, peas, and carrots. Cook over low heat for 30 minutes, adding a little water if necessary.

UNCLE DAVID'S LAMB AND RICE

2 tablespoons shortening
2 onions, chopped
6 shoulder lamb chops
1 tablespoon salt
½ teaspoon freshly ground black pepper
1 bay leaf
2 carrots, sliced
2 stalks celery, chopped
6 cups water
1 cup rice
¼ pound mushrooms, chopped
2 egg yolks, beaten

Heat the shortening in a heavy saucepan or casserole. Add the onions and lamb chops. Cook over medium heat for 15 minutes, turning the chops frequently. Add the salt, pepper, bay leaf, carrots, celery, and water. Cook over medium heat for 30 minutes. Remove the chops. Add the rice and mushrooms. Cover and cook over low heat for 25 minutes. Discard the bay leaf. Add the egg yolks, stirring constantly to prevent curdling. Place the chops on top.
Bake uncovered in a 375° oven for 10 minutes.

ARMENIAN-STYLE LAMB CHOPS

2 cloves garlic, minced
½ cup lemon juice
2 teaspoons salt
½ teaspoon freshly ground black
   pepper
1 teaspoon paprika
6–12 lamb chops, trimmed

Combine the garlic, lemon juice, salt, pepper, and paprika in a bowl. Marinate the chops in this mixture for at least 2 hours, basting and turning them frequently.

Broil in a very hot oven to desired degree of rareness.

LAMB AND LIMA BEANS

1½ cups dried lima beans
2 tablespoons olive oil
2 pounds boneless lamb, cubed
2 onions, chopped
1 clove garlic, minced
½ teaspoon freshly ground black
   pepper
1 bay leaf
2 tomatoes, chopped
2½ cups water
2½ teaspoons salt

Wash the beans thoroughly. Place in a saucepan; cover with water; bring to a boil and let soak for 2 hours. Drain.

Heat the oil in a heavy saucepan. Brown the lamb in it. Add the onions, garlic, pepper, bay leaf, tomatoes, water, and beans. Cover and cook over low heat 2 hours. Add the salt and a little water if necessary. Cook for 30 minutes longer, or until beans are tender. Remove bay leaf and discard. Correct seasoning.

When I make this recipe I double everything and I also use two pots. One for the actual dinner and one for the tasting. As soon as I start to cook my Stuffed Cabbage I am descended on. From all four corners of the house my family comes in for a taste. Can I be cruel and say no? Of course not! So that's why I make a double recipe, and after you try this Stuffed Cabbage I am sure that you will be in my same trouble.

HOLISHKES

STUFFED CABBAGE

1 large head cabbage
Beef bones
1 can (⅜2½) tomatoes
2 onions, chopped
1 pound ground beef
1 onion, grated
3 teaspoons salt
¼ teaspoon freshly ground black
   pepper
½ cup rice, half cooked and
   drained
1 egg, beaten
4 tablespoons lemon juice
3 tablespoons brown sugar

Pour boiling water over the cabbage and cook for 10 minutes. Drain well. Carefully separate the leaves of the cabbage so as to obtain 12 large leaves.

Combine the beef bones, tomatoes, and chopped onions in a heavy saucepan. Cook over medium heat while preparing the *holishkes*.

Mix the beef, grated onion, 1½ teaspoons of the salt, the pepper, rice, and egg. Mix until well blended. Place a heaping tablespoon of the mixture on each cabbage leaf. Tuck the opposite sides in and carefully roll up the cabbage leaf. (If necessary, fasten each end with toothpicks, or tie with white thread.) Carefully place them in the tomato mixture with the remaining salt. Cover and cook over low heat for 1 hour. Add the lemon juice and sugar. Cook uncovered for 30 minutes. Correct seasoning. The sauce should be both sweet and sour, so add additional lemon juice or sugar if necessary. Serve hot.

SWEET AND SOUR MEAT BALLS

3 tablespoons cold water
2 tablespoons bread crumbs
2 pounds ground beef
1 onion, grated
3 teaspoons salt
½ teaspoon freshly ground black pepper
2 eggs, beaten
3 tablespoons shortening
2 onions, sliced
1½ cups boiling water
3 tablespoons sugar
¼ cup seedless raisins
1 tablespoon vinegar
1 lemon, sliced thin
2 gingersnaps, crushed

Mix the cold water and bread crumbs together. Add to the meat, together with the grated onion, 2 teaspoons of the salt, the pepper, and eggs. Mix well. Form into 1-inch balls.

Melt the shortening in a saucepan. Add the sliced onions and meat balls. Cook over medium heat until browned. Add the boiling water, sugar, raisins, vinegar, lemon slices, and remaining salt. Cover and cook over low heat for 20 minutes. Add the gingersnaps, stirring until smooth. Cook for 5 minutes additional. Correct seasoning.

MEAT AND CABBAGE

4 pounds beef (brisket, short ribs,
  or chuck)
3 onions, chopped
1 can (※2) tomatoes
2½ teaspoons salt
½ teaspoon freshly ground black
  pepper
1 head cabbage (about 4
  pounds), coarsely shredded
1 apple, peeled and grated
⅓ cup lemon juice
4 tablespoons sugar

Brown the beef and onions in a heavy skillet or Dutch oven. Add the tomatoes, salt, and pepper. Cover and cook over low heat for 1½ hours. Add the cabbage and apple. Cook for 45 minutes additional. Add the lemon juice and sugar, and cook for 15 minutes. Correct seasoning, adding more lemon juice or sugar to give the dish both a sweet and sour flavor.

Continue cooking for an additional 30 minutes, or until the meat is tender. Slice the meat and serve with the cabbage.

MY TURKISH NEIGHBOR'S BEEF
& EGGPLANT CASSEROLE

6 tablespoons olive oil
2 pounds beef, cubed small
2½ teaspoons salt
¾ teaspoon freshly ground black
  pepper
1 eggplant, sliced thin
2 onions, sliced thin
4 tomatoes, chopped
2 green peppers

Heat 3 tablespoons of the oil in a skillet. Brown the beef in it. Mix the salt and pepper together.

In a greased casserole arrange successive layers of the eggplant, beef, onions, tomatoes, and green peppers, sprinkling with the salt and pepper. Make as many layers as possible. Sprinkle the remaining olive oil over the top. Cover the casserole.

Bake in a 350° oven for 1 hour. Remove the cover and bake 15 minutes longer.

STUFFED PEPPERS

6 green peppers
1 pound ground beef
¼ cup uncooked rice
3 onions
3 teaspoons salt
½ teaspoon freshly ground black
    pepper
1 egg, beaten
3 tablespoons cold water
3 tablespoons shortening
1 can (※2½) tomatoes
1 beef bone
4 tablespoons brown sugar
4 tablespoons lemon juice

Place the peppers in a saucepan with water to cover. Bring to a boil. Remove from heat and let soak for 5 minutes. Drain and cool. Cut a 1-inch piece across the top of the stem end of the peppers and reserve. Remove the fibers and seeds.

Mix the beef and rice together. Grate 1 onion and add, together with 1½ teaspoons of the salt, ¼ teaspoon of the pepper, the egg, and water. Mix well. Stuff the peppers. Replace the tops firmly.

Melt the shortening in a saucepan. Slice the remaining onions and sauté for 10 minutes, stirring frequently. Place the peppers over them. Add the tomatoes, beef bone, remaining salt and pepper. Cover and cook over low heat for 1 hour. Add the brown sugar and lemon juice, and stir. Cook 30 minutes longer, or until peppers are tender. Correct seasoning.

STUFFED DERMA (CASING)

> 1 beef casing (about 12–15 inches in length)
> 1 cup sifted flour
> 3 tablespoons matzo or cracker meal
> 1 teaspoon salt
> ¼ teaspoon freshly ground black pepper
> 1½ teaspoons paprika
> 1 onion, grated
> ½ cup melted shortening
> 4 tablespoons shortening
> 2 onions, sliced

Wash the *derma* thoroughly in cold water. Scrape thoroughly, inside and out. Wash again in warm water. Dry. Sew one end of the *derma*.

Mix the flour, matzo meal, salt, pepper, paprika, and grated onion together. Add the melted shortening and mix well. Stuff the *derma* lightly. Sew the open end. Place in boiling water for 2 minutes. Remove carefully.

Place the 4 tablespoons of shortening and the sliced onions in a baking dish. Place the *derma* on top.

Roast in a 350° oven for 2 hours, basting frequently. Slice about ¾ inch thick and serve hot with meat or poultry. If desired, the *derma* may be placed in the roasting pan when roasting chicken, duck, or beef.

Some nights I have a previous with the P.T.A. And on those days Jake stays late at the factory, so I prepare this recipe for him to cook when he gets home. It's very simple and all Jake needs is a match and before you know it, 1, 2, 3.

There's supper all good and hot and tasty—at least I haven't had a complaint yet, but maybe that's because Jake is so glad to see me home at long last.

JAKE'S DO-IT-YOURSELF SUPPER (FOR P.T.A. NIGHTS)

4 tablespoons salad oil
1 onion, chopped
1 clove garlic, minced
1 pound green beans cut in 2-inch pieces, or 1 package frozen
2 cups canned tomatoes, drained
3 teaspoons salt
½ teaspoon pepper
1 bay leaf
½ teaspoon orégano
1 pound chopped beef
½ pound mushrooms, sliced
½ pound calf's liver, cubed

Heat 2 tablespoons of the oil in a saucepan. Add the onion, garlic, beans, tomatoes, 2 teaspoons salt, ¼ teaspoon pepper, the bay leaf, and orégano. Cover and cook over low heat for 45 minutes.

Mix the beef and remaining salt and pepper together; shape into walnut-sized balls. Heat remaining oil in a skillet; brown the balls in it. Add to the beans with the mushrooms; cook 5 minutes. Brown the liver in the oil remaining in the skillet and add to the beans. Cook 5 minutes. Correct seasoning and serve.

SURPRISE MEAT PIE

2 cups sifted flour
2 teaspoons salt
1 cup shortening
2 egg yolks
3 tablespoons ice water
2 teaspoons salad oil
3 onions, chopped
1½ pounds ground beef
2 teaspoons caraway seeds
½ cup seedless raisins
3 hard-cooked eggs, coarsely
    chopped
12 ripe olives, sliced

Sift the flour and ½ teaspoon of the salt into a bowl. Cut in the shortening with a pastry blender or two knives until the mixture has the consistency of coarse sand. Beat the egg yolks and ice water together and add, tossing until a ball of dough is formed. Chill for 1 hour and prepare the filling.

Heat the oil in a skillet. Sauté the onions and beef in it for 10 minutes, stirring frequently. Add the caraway seeds, raisins, chopped eggs, olives, and remaining salt. Mix well. Cool for 45 minutes.

Preheat oven to 375°. Divide the dough into two parts, one slightly larger than the other. Roll out the larger piece to fit an 11-inch pie plate. Pour the meat mixture into it. Roll out the remaining dough and cover, sealing the edges well. Slash the top in two places. Bake for 35 minutes, or until delicately browned on top.

Serve hot, in pie-shaped pieces.

Vegetables

Healthy! That's what this section is, healthy. Not that meat and soups and poultry are not healthy, but they don't have the vitamins and minerals the vegetables have. Of course vitamins and minerals never made My Sammy eat vegetables. "For rabbits," he said, and he wouldn't eat. So I asked my neighbors, "How should I make My Sammy eat his vegetables?" and each one said, "Cook them my way" or "Make them like I make them" . . . and lo and behold, after I tried these recipes Sammy eats his vegetables, and even asks for them. If you have my old trouble try these recipes because they will surely solve your problem. Also, if you don't have any troubles you can try them for a change.

RICE-STUFFED PEPPERS

4 tablespoons butter
4 onions, chopped
2½ cups rice, half cooked and
  drained
3 teaspoons salt
½ teaspoon freshly ground black
  pepper
2 tablespoons chopped parsley
1 carrot, grated
2 scallions (green onions),
  chopped
1 egg
6 large green peppers
1 tablespoon flour
1½ cups canned tomato sauce
½ cup water
2 teaspoons sugar
1 cup sour cream

Melt the butter in a saucepan. Add the onions. Sauté for 10 minutes, stirring frequently. Remove half the onions and combine with the rice, 1 teaspoon of the salt, ¼ teaspoon of the pepper, the parsley, carrot, scallions, and egg. Mix well.

Cut a 1-inch slice from the stem end of the peppers. Carefully remove the seeds and fibers. Pour boiling water over the peppers and allow to soak for 5 minutes. Drain well. Stuff with the rice mixture.

Sprinkle the flour on the onions remaining in the saucepan. Cook, stirring constantly, until brown. Add the tomato sauce, water, sugar, and remaining salt and pepper. Mix well. Place the peppers upright, open end up, in the saucepan. Cover and cook over low heat for 45 minutes, or until the peppers are tender. Baste frequently.

Add the sour cream to the sauce, and stir. Serve hot.

CARROT STICKS IN HONEY

3 tablespoons shortening
9 carrots, scraped and cut into
  quarters
2 tablespoons water
¼ cup honey
1½ teaspoons salt
¼ teaspoon nutmeg

Melt the shortening in a saucepan. Add the carrots, water, honey, salt, and nutmeg. Cover and cook over low heat for 20 minutes, or until carrots are tender. Stir gently but frequently.

BEETS AND PRUNES

1 pound unsweetened prunes,
  presoaked
6 beets, cooked, peeled, and
  grated
1½ cups water
⅓ cup sugar
1 tablespoon lemon juice
½ teaspoon salt

Combine the prunes, beets, water, sugar, lemon juice, and salt in a saucepan. Cook over low heat for 30 minutes. Correct seasoning, adding a little more sugar if too tart.

Serve with meat dishes.

Sometimes it's hard to decide on what to have for a vegetable. After all, every family has its likes and dislikes, and my family is very definite. So when the mood is upon them and vegetables is not the order of the day I make this Carrot Pudding. Does it work? I should so say so, and you won't be disappointed either.

CARROT PUDDING

6 egg yolks
¾ cup sugar
8 carrots, peeled and grated
  (about 2 cups)
⅓ cup matzo meal
¼ cup potato starch
½ teaspoon salt
⅓ cup sweet red wine
1 tablespoon lemon juice
2 teaspoons grated lemon rind
6 egg whites

Beat the egg yolks. Add the sugar, beating until thick, and light in color. Add the carrots, matzo meal, potato starch, and salt. Mix well. Add the wine, lemon juice, and lemon rind. Mix. Preheat oven to 375°.

Beat the egg whites until stiff but not dry. Fold into the carrot mixture carefully. Pour into a greased 2-quart casserole or baking dish.

Bake for 45 minutes. Serve hot or cold as a vegetable.

POTATO CHARLOTTE

3 carrots, grated
¾ cup water
5 potatoes, peeled, grated, and
    drained
¼ cup matzo meal or cracker
    meal
3 egg yolks
2 teaspoons salt
¼ teaspoon freshly ground black
    pepper
1 teaspoon sugar
¼ cup melted shortening
3 egg whites, stiffly beaten

Combine the carrots and water in a saucepan. Bring to a boil. Cook over medium heat for 10 minutes. Cool, but do not drain. Preheat oven to 350°.

Mix the undrained carrots with the potatoes, matzo meal, egg yolks, salt, pepper, sugar, and shortening. Fold in the egg whites thoroughly. Pour into a greased 1½-quart casserole.

Bake for 1 hour, or until set and browned on top. Serve as a vegetable or as a luncheon dish.

EGGS AND POTATOES

4 potatoes, peeled, boiled, and
   sliced
6 hard-cooked eggs, sliced
1 cup sour cream
4 tablespoons butter
2 teaspoons salt
¼ teaspoon freshly ground black
   pepper
½ teaspoon paprika

Using half of the above ingredients, line a buttered casserole with successive layers of potatoes, eggs, sour cream. Dot with half the butter, and sprinkle with half of the salt, pepper, and paprika. Repeat, using up the balance of the ingredients.

Bake in a 350° oven for 35 minutes. Serve as a luncheon dish or for a light supper. It may also be served as an accompaniment to a fish course.

STUFFED POTATO BALLS

4 cups mashed potatoes
2 eggs
¼ cup cracker or matzo meal
1½ teaspoons salt
½ teaspoon freshly ground black
   pepper
¾ cup ground cooked beef,
   chicken, or liver
2 teaspoons grated onion
2 tablespoons melted shortening
Fat for deep frying

Mix the potatoes, eggs, cracker meal, ½ teaspoon of the salt, and

¼ teaspoon of the pepper together until smooth. Break into 12 pieces. Pat each one down on a lightly floured board.

Mix the beef, onion, shortening, and remaining salt and pepper together. Place 1 teaspoonful of the mixture on each piece of dough, and pinch the edges together to form a ball.

Heat the fat to 370° and drop the balls into it. Fry until browned. Drain. Serve instead of potatoes. If desired, smaller versions of these potato balls may be made and served as *hors d'oeuvres*.

STUFFED POTATOES

6 Idaho potatoes, baked
2 teaspoons salt
¼ teaspoon freshly ground black
    pepper
4 tablespoons butter
4 tablespoons sour cream
4 tablespoons cottage cheese
1 egg
1 tablespoon chopped chives,
    scallions, or onions (optional)

Cut the top third lengthwise off the potatoes. Remove the pulp and mash, but reserve the shells. Add the salt, pepper, butter, sour cream, cottage cheese, egg, and chives. Beat together until light and fluffy. Stuff the shells.

Bake in a 425° oven for 10 minutes.

Chanukah *is the Festival of the Lights, and everybody exchanges gifts. It lasts for eight days and each day another candle is lit on the eight-branched candelabra to celebrate* the recapture of the Temple by Judas Maccabeus. When the Temple was taken back from the Syrian King there was only enough holy oil so that the candelabra could be lit for one day, but there was a miracle and the candelabra burned for eight days. Maccabeus made this a holiday and that is why it is called the Festival of the Lights.

I don't know why my potato kugel always seems right for Chanukah—*maybe because it's light. Try it.*

POTATO KUGEL (PUDDING)

6 potatoes
1 onion, grated
2 egg yolks, beaten
4 tablespoons cracker or matzo
    meal
1 teaspoon baking powder
1½ teaspoons salt
¼ teaspoon freshly ground black
    pepper
4 tablespoons melted butter or
    chicken fat
2 egg whites, stiffly beaten

Peel and grate the potatoes into salted water. Preheat oven to 375°.

Drain the potatoes well. Combine in a bowl with the onion, egg yolks, cracker meal, baking powder, salt, pepper, and 2 tablespoons of the shortening. Mix together well. Fold in the egg whites carefully but thoroughly.

Pour the mixture into a greased 1½-quart baking dish. Pour the remaining shortening on top.

Bake in a 375° oven for 1 hour, or until the mixture is set and lightly browned on top.

Serve with meat, poultry, or fish dishes.

RICE KUGEL (PUDDING)

1½ cups rice
4 cups water
1½ teaspoons salt
6 eggs
⅓ cup sugar
½ cup seedless raisins
⅓ cup melted shortening

Combine the rice, water, and salt in a saucepan. Cover, bring to a boil, and cook for 10 minutes. Drain any remaining liquid. Preheat oven to 375°.

Beat the eggs and sugar together. Add the rice, raisins, and shortening. Mix well. Pour into a well-greased 2-quart casserole.

Bake for 30 minutes, or until set and browned. Cut into squares and serve hot in place of potatoes.

CABBAGE KUGEL (PUDDING)

4 tablespoons shortening
4 cups finely shredded cabbage
6 slices white bread, trimmed
1 cup boiling water
½ cup sifted flour
½ cup ground blanched almonds
¼ cup white raisins
1 teaspoon salt
2 teaspoons lemon juice
4 egg yolks
4 egg whites, stiffly beaten

Melt the shortening in a skillet. Add the cabbage and cook over low heat for 45 minutes, stirring very frequently. Chill for 3 hours.

Soak the bread in the water for 5 minutes. Drain and mash. Mix the flour, almonds, raisins, salt, lemon juice, egg yolks, and the bread until very smooth. Add the cabbage; mix lightly. Fold in the egg whites carefully but thoroughly. Pour into a greased baking dish or casserole.

Bake in a 350° oven for 35 minutes, or until browned and set.

BARLEY KUGEL (PUDDING)

> 4 cups stock or canned con-
> sommé
> 1¼ cups pearl barley
> 1 teaspoon salt
> ¼ teaspoon pepper
> 1 cup chopped mushrooms
> 2 eggs, beaten

Bring the stock to a boil in a saucepan. Add barley, salt, and pepper, stirring constantly. Cook over medium heat for 10 minutes, stirring occasionally. Cover and cook over low heat 45 minutes. Add the mushrooms and cook 10 minutes longer, or until barley is thick and soft. Preheat oven to 350°.

Add the barley to the eggs, mixing steadily to prevent curdling. Pour into a greased baking dish.

Bake 35 minutes, or until set and lightly browned.

Serve with any meat or poultry dish.

Succoth is known as the Festival of the Tabernacles, and a succoth is a small hut covered with vines and leaves. Inside, the walls and the ceiling are covered with fruits and vegetables. Like Thanksgiving, Succoth is a holiday that celebrates the harvest. I am always surprised when My

Sammy tells me that every country and every religion of the whole world has a holiday something like Succoth. But then I think, why not? Why not? Since everybody is people, so why shouldn't everybody have the same kind of a holiday? And be thankful for all the good things God gave us?

It's funny the way certain dishes become a favorite for certain holidays. Well, the Cabbage Strudel is my favorite— but I'll tell you a secret, I make it when the mood overcomes me, holiday or not!

CABBAGE STRUDEL

2½ cups sifted flour
½ teaspoon baking powder
2 teaspoons salt
1 egg
6 tablespoons salad oil
¾ cup ice water
½ cup chicken fat or butter
6 cups finely grated cabbage
1 onion, chopped
¼ teaspoon freshly ground black
    pepper
½ teaspoon sugar

Sift the flour, baking powder, and ½ teaspoon of the salt into a bowl. Make a well in the center. Place the egg, 4 tablespoons of the salad oil, and the ice water in it. Work in the flour until a dough is formed. If too soft, add a little more flour. Knead until smooth and elastic. Cover the dough with a warm bowl while preparing the filling.

Melt the shortening in a skillet. Add the cabbage, onion, pepper, sugar, and remaining salt. Sauté for 20 minutes, stirring frequently. Cool for 20 minutes. Preheat oven to 350°.

Roll out the dough as thin as possible on a lightly floured surface. Spread the cabbage mixture on it. Roll up carefully, as for a jelly roll. Place on a greased, shallow baking pan. Brush with the remaining salad oil.

Bake for 45 minutes, or until crisp and brown. Slice the *strudel* while hot. Very small versions of this dish are excellent for *hors d'oeuvres*.

SAUERKRAUT FILLING FOR STRUDEL

3 tablespoons shortening
1½ pounds sauerkraut, drained
    and chopped
3 tablespoons grated onion
½ teaspoon freshly ground black
    pepper
1 teaspoon sugar

Melt the shortening in a skillet. Add the sauerkraut and onion. Sauté for 10 minutes, stirring frequently. Add the pepper and sugar. Mix well together and let cool.

Proceed as directed above, in place of the cabbage filling.

CARROT TZIMMES

2 tablespoons fine barley
4 tablespoons shortening
4 cups grated carrots
2 apples, peeled and grated
1 teaspoon salt
2 teaspoons sugar
½ cup water

Soak the barley in water to cover for 2 hours. Drain well.

Combine the shortening, carrots, apples, salt, sugar, and water in a saucepan. Add the barley and mix together. Cover and cook over low heat for 2 hours, or until the barley is tender. Stir frequently, adding more water if necessary.

Serve hot, as a vegetable.

To define tzimmes would be a presumption. It's a word that means many things and mostly it means a lot of things mixed together. In non-cooking it means a lot of people making a lot of noise, or one person making a fuss. In this case it's very definite. It's made of a lot of things and pumpkin, and there is no two ways about this recipe. It's a delicious tzimmes.

PUMPKIN TZIMMES

4 pounds pumpkin (or yellow
    squash), peeled and diced
2 tablespoons rice
1½ teaspoons salt
2 teaspoons sugar
4 tablespoons butter
½ cup sour cream

Combine the pumpkin, rice, and salt in a saucepan. Cook over low heat for 45 minutes. Mix frequently. (It is not usually necessary to add water, as the vegetable has its own.)

Mash the mixture until smooth. Add the sugar, butter, and cream. Cook over low heat for 10 minutes, stirring occasionally. Correct seasoning.

Serve as a vegetable.

RED CABBAGE,
SWEET AND SOUR STYLE

2 tablespoons shortening
3 pounds red cabbage, finely
    shredded
½ cup water
1½ teaspoons salt
¼ teaspoon freshly ground black
    pepper
2 tablespoons flour
4 tablespoons cider vinegar
3 tablespoons brown sugar

Melt the shortening in a saucepan. Add the cabbage, water, salt, and pepper. Cover and cook over low heat for 1 hour. Mix the flour and vinegar to a smooth paste and add, together with the brown sugar. Cook for 5 minutes, stirring almost constantly. Correct seasoning, adding vinegar and sugar if necessary. There should be pronounced flavors of both sweet and sour.

Serve with roast poultry or with meat dishes.

NOTE: The flavor will be improved if the dish is prepared several hours before it is to be used, and then reheated.

SWEET AND SOUR STRING BEANS

2 pounds fresh string beans, cut
    in half, or 2 packages frozen
2 teaspoons salt
3 cups water
3 tablespoons shortening
2 tablespoons flour
3 tablespoons sugar
3 tablespoons vinegar

146

Combine the beans, salt, and water in a saucepan. Bring to a boil. Cook over medium heat for 10 minutes. Drain, reserving 1½ cups of the stock.

Melt the shortening in the saucepan. Add the flour, stirring until smooth. Add the stock, stirring constantly until the boiling point. Add the sugar, vinegar, and beans. Cover and cook over low heat for 15 minutes. Correct seasoning.

MEATLESS HOLISHKES

STUFFED CABBAGE

1 head cabbage
2 cups half-cooked rice
4 tablespoons bread crumbs
1 onion, grated
2 teaspoons salt
½ teaspoon freshly ground black pepper
2 eggs, beaten
1½ cups seedless raisins
6 tablespoons shortening
3 onions, sliced
2 tablespoons flour
2 cups boiling water
¼ cup lemon juice
1 teaspoon cinnamon

Carefully separate the leaves of cabbage. Pour boiling water over them and let soak for 15 minutes. Mix the rice, bread crumbs, grated onion, 1 teaspoon of the salt, ¼ teaspoon of the pepper, the eggs, and ¾ cup of the raisins together. Mix well. Place a heaping tablespoon of the mixture on each cabbage leaf, turn in the sides, and roll up carefully. Fasten the ends with toothpicks or tie with white thread if necessary.

Melt half of the shortening in a skillet. Brown the *holishkes* in it. Transfer carefully to a baking dish. Melt the remaining half of the shortening in the skillet. Add the sliced onions. Sauté for 10 minutes, stirring frequently. Add the flour. Cook, stirring constantly, until brown. Add the water, stirring constantly until the boiling point. Add the lemon juice, cinnamon, remaining salt, pepper, and raisins. Pour the mixture over the *holishkes*.

Bake in a 350° oven for 1 hour. Baste frequently. Correct seasoning, adding a little more lemon juice or sugar if necessary.

Serve as a main course, or as a vegetable with plain roast meats or poultry.

ZWIEBELKUCHEN

ONION TART

1 cup sifted flour
½ teaspoon salt
¼ pound butter
2 tablespoons sour cream

Sift the flour and salt into a bowl. Work the butter in by hand. Add the sour cream, mixing until a ball of dough is formed. Chill for 2 hours. Now prepare the filling:

3 tablespoons butter
6 onions, sliced thin
2 teaspoons salt
2 eggs
1 cup sour cream
¼ teaspoon white pepper
1 teaspoon paprika

Melt the butter in a skillet. Sauté the onions in it for 10 minutes, but do not allow them to brown. Add 1 teaspoon of the salt, and mix.

Roll out the dough on a lightly floured surface to fit a 9-inch pie plate, and line the pie plate with the dough. Flute the edges. Place the onions in it. Preheat oven to 400°.

Beat the eggs, sour cream, pepper, paprika, and remaining salt together and pour over the onions.

Bake in a 400° oven for 10 minutes. Reduce heat to 350° and bake for 20 minutes longer, or until a knife comes out clean.

Serve as an appetizer or as an accompaniment to a main course. Serve hot.

STUFFED ONION PASTRY

> 1½ cups sifted flour
> ½ teaspoon salt
> ¾ cup shortening
> 1 egg
> 2 tablespoons ice water

Sift the flour and salt into a bowl. Cut in the shortening with a pastry blender or 2 knives. Beat the eggs and water together and add, tossing lightly until a ball of dough is formed. Chill for 1 hour. Now prepare the filling:

> ¼ cup butter or chicken fat
> 10 onions, sliced thin
> 1½ teaspoons salt
> ½ teaspoon freshly ground black
>   pepper
> ¼ teaspoon sugar
> ¼ cup melted butter or chicken
>   fat

Melt the ¼ cup shortening in a skillet. Add the onions, salt, pepper, and sugar. Sauté for 15 minutes, stirring frequently. Correct seasoning. Cool for 15 minutes.

Preheat oven to 375°. Roll out the dough as thin as possible on a lightly floured surface.

Brush the dough with the ¼ cup melted shortening and cover with the onions. Roll up and place on a greased baking sheet.

Bake for 35 minutes, or until browned. Slice and serve hot.

ONION PUDDING

6 egg yolks
4 onions, finely chopped
⅓ cup matzo meal
1½ teaspoons salt
¼ teaspoon freshly ground black
   pepper
⅓ cup melted shortening
6 egg whites

Beat the egg yolks in a bowl. Add the onions, matzo meal, salt, pepper, and shortening. Mix well. Preheat oven to 350°.

Beat the egg whites until stiff but not dry. Fold them into the onion mixture. Pour into a greased 2-quart casserole or baking dish.

Bake for 40 minutes.

Serve as a vegetable.

ONIONS AND LIMA BEANS

4 tablespoons shortening
12 whole small white onions, or
   3 onions, sliced
1 tablespoon flour
1 cup water
1 bay leaf
2 peppercorns
1½ teaspoons salt
¼ teaspoon freshly ground black
   pepper
2 pounds lima beans, shelled, or
   1 package frozen

Melt the shortening in a saucepan. Add the onions. Sauté for 15 minutes, stirring frequently. Sprinkle the flour over them and mix.

Add the water, stirring constantly to the boiling point. Add the bay leaf, peppercorns, salt, and pepper. Cover and cook over low heat for 10 minutes. Add the lima beans. Cover and cook over low heat for 15 minutes, or until beans are tender. Mix frequently to prevent burning.

BAKED ONION DUMPLINGS

> 1½ cups sifted flour
> 2 teaspoons salt
> 1 cup shortening
> 1 egg yolk
> 4 tablespoons ice water
> 6 large onions (Bermuda, if available)
> 2 cups stock or canned consommé
> ½ teaspoon freshly ground black pepper

Sift the flour and ½ teaspoon of the salt into a bowl. Cut in the shortening (reserving 2 tablespoons) with a pastry blender or 2 knives. Beat the egg yolk and water together and add, tossing lightly until a ball of dough is formed. Chill for 1 hour.

Combine the onions, stock, and remaining shortening in a saucepan. Bring to a boil and cook over low heat for 20 minutes, or until onions are tender but firm. Drain well. Cool for 1 hour. Sprinkle with the pepper and remaining salt. Preheat oven to 375°.

Roll out the dough ⅛ inch thick on a lightly floured surface. Cut 6 pieces large enough to cover the onions. Place an onion on each, pinching edges together. Place on a baking sheet.

Bake for 25 minutes, or until browned. Serve with roasts, poultry, or fish dishes.

ZWIEBELAUFLAUF

BAKED ONION
CUSTARD

6 onions, sliced
½ cup milk
2 tablespoons butter
3 egg yolks
½ cup sour cream
1 teaspoon salt
⅛ teaspoon white pepper
3 tablespoons bread crumbs
3 tablespoons grated gruyère
    cheese

Combine the onions, milk, and butter in a saucepan. Cook over low heat for 15 minutes. Drain. Place onions in a buttered baking dish. Preheat oven to 350°.

Beat the egg yolks, sour cream, salt, and pepper together; pour over the onions. Sprinkle with the bread crumbs and cheese.

Bake 20 minutes, or until set and lightly browned. Serve directly from the baking dish.

MUSHROOMS ON TOAST

4 tablespoons butter
1 onion, chopped
1 pound mushrooms, washed,
    drained, and sliced
1 teaspoon salt
¼ teaspoon freshly ground black
    pepper
¾ cup sour cream
6 slices white toast

Melt the butter in a skillet. Add the onion. Sauté for 5 minutes, stirring frequently. Add the mushrooms. Cover and cook over low heat for 15 minutes. Remove the cover and cook until almost all the liquid evaporates, about 2 minutes. Add the salt, pepper, and sour cream. Mix well. Cook for 3 minutes.

Serve over toast as a vegetable course or as a first course.

BEETS, POLISH STYLE

6 beets, peeled
2 tablespoons lemon juice
3 tablespoons butter
2 tablespoons flour
1 cup light cream
1 teaspoon salt

Place the beets in a saucepan with cold water to cover. Add the lemon juice. Cook over medium heat for 25 minutes, or until the beets are tender. Drain. Cool. Grate the beets.

Melt the butter in a saucepan. Add the flour, stirring until smooth. Gradually add the cream, stirring constantly until the boiling point. Add the beets and salt. Mix. Cook over low heat for 5 minutes.

CHICK-PEAS AND RICE

2 cups water
1 teaspoon salt
½ cup rice
1½ cups cooked chick-peas
⅓ cup honey
⅓ cup brown sugar

Combine the water, salt, and rice in a saucepan. Cover, bring to a boil, and cook over low heat for 12 minutes. Pour into a casserole. Add the chick-peas, honey, and brown sugar.

Bake in a 350° oven for 25 minutes.

Serve as a vegetable.

BAKED NAHIT

BAKED CHICK-PEAS

1 pound chick-peas
2 teaspoons salt
¼ teaspoon freshly ground black pepper
3 tablespoons shortening
½ cup honey
½ cup water

Wash the chick-peas. Cover with water and let soak overnight. Drain. Add fresh water to cover. Bring to a boil. Cover and cook over low heat for 1¼ hours, or until almost tender. Drain, sprinkle with the salt and pepper, and mix gently.

Melt the shortening in a casserole. Add the chick-peas. Combine the honey and water and pour over the chick-peas.

Bake in a 375° oven for 25 minutes.

Serve as a vegetable.

CABBAGE WITH SOUR CREAM

4 tablespoons butter
1 head cabbage (about 4
   pounds), shredded
1½ teaspoons salt
¼ teaspoon freshly ground black
   pepper
2 tablespoons sugar
1 egg
1 cup sour cream
2 tablespoons lemon juice

Melt the butter in a large skillet. Add the cabbage. Sauté for 15 minutes, stirring frequently, but do not allow the cabbage to brown. Add the salt, pepper, and sugar. Cook over low heat for 10 minutes without browning.

Beat the egg, sour cream, and lemon juice together. Pour over the cabbage, stirring constantly. Heat, but do not allow to boil.

BAKED LIMA BEANS WITH HONEY

2 cups dried lima beans
3 tablespoons shortening
2 onions, chopped
2 teaspoons salt
¾ cup honey

Wash the beans thoroughly. Place in a saucepan with water to cover. Bring to a boil; remove from the heat and let soak for 1½ hours. Drain. Cover with fresh water. Bring to a boil, cover, and cook over medium heat for 2 hours. Drain if any liquid remains.

Melt the shortening in a skillet. Add the onions and sauté for 15 minutes, stirring frequently. Combine the beans, onions, salt, and honey and mix well. Place in casserole.

Bake in a 350° oven for 1 hour, or until the beans are tender and glazed.

Serve with meat dishes.

PEAS IN SOUR CREAM

3 pounds or 2 packages frozen
  green peas, cooked and drained
1 tablespoon butter
2 teaspoons chopped chives or
  scallions (green onions)
1 cup sour cream

Combine the peas, butter, and chives in a saucepan. Place over low heat until butter melts. Add the sour cream; heat, but do not allow to boil. Correct seasoning.

Salads &
Relishes

Salads and relishes are taken for granted. It goes without saying that when you set a table you also set out a salad and a relish or two. Try once not serving them and see what happens. If sometimes in my haste I forget one or the other the family is sure I'm sick or something has happened. So if by a perchance the same situation is in your home and you wish to put your family at ease, try some of these recipes. Not only will they notice the taste, but they will be assured of your health.

PICKLED STUFFED PEPPERS

12 green peppers
4 cups shredded cabbage
2 cucumbers, chopped
2 sweet red peppers, chopped
2 onions, chopped
1 tablespoon salt
2 tablespoons celery seeds
2 tablespoons prepared horseradish
12 cloves garlic
1½ quarts cider vinegar

Cut a 1-inch slice from the stem end of the peppers and reserve. Remove the seeds and fibers.

Mix together the cabbage, cucumbers, red peppers, onions, salt, celery seeds, and horseradish. Stuff the peppers with the mixture. Place a clove of garlic in each. Replace the tops of the peppers and fasten with toothpicks.

Pack the peppers into sterilized jars. Fill to overflowing with the vinegar. (If necessary, use more vinegar than the amount specified.) Seal the jars.

Store in a dark, cool place for at least 2 weeks before using.

LETTUCE SALAD WITH SOUR CREAM

1 cup sour cream
2 tablespoons lemon juice
1 tablespoon vinegar
2 tablespoons grated onion
1 clove garlic, minced
1 teaspoon salt
¼ teaspoon white pepper
2 heads lettuce, washed and drained
2 hard-cooked eggs, sliced

Mix the sour cream, lemon juice, vinegar, onion, garlic, salt, and pepper together.

Separate leaves from the heads of lettuce and dry thoroughly. Pour dressing over them. Place in the refrigerator for 2 hours. Add the eggs and serve.

PICKLED PEPPER SALAD

6 green peppers
1 cup vinegar
⅓ cup water
1 bay leaf
1 teaspoon salt
1 teaspoon sugar
Dash cayenne pepper
1 clove garlic, minced

Cut the peppers in half. Remove the fibers and seeds. Place the peppers under a hot broiler, as close to the heat as possible. Broil until the skins brown. Remove and peel. Cool. Cut each half of pepper in half.

Combine the vinegar, water, bay leaf, salt, sugar, and cayenne pepper. Boil for 2 minutes. Cool.

Place the peppers in a bowl or glass jar. Add the garlic. Pour the vinegar mixture over the peppers. Chill for at least 3 hours before serving.

Serve as a salad or as a relish.

CABBAGE SALAD

> 2 pounds cabbage
> 2 carrots
> 1 green pepper, cut into julienne strips
> 2 teaspoons salt
> 1 cup cider vinegar
> ½ cup water
> 1 tablespoon sugar
> ¼ teaspoon freshly ground black pepper
> 1 teaspoon celery seeds (optional)

Grate or shred the cabbage very fine. Grate the carrots. Combine the cabbage, carrots, green pepper, and salt in a large bowl. Toss. Set aside for 10 minutes.

Mix the vinegar, water, sugar, black pepper, and celery seeds together. Pour over the cabbage and toss well. Chill for 1 hour.

RED CABBAGE SLAW

4 cups boiling water
4 cups shredded red cabbage
2 tablespoons vinegar
1 tablespoon salt
1 apple, peeled and grated
1 onion, grated
3 tablespoons lemon juice
3 tablespoons salad oil
⅛ teaspoon freshly ground black
pepper

Pour the boiling water over the cabbage. Add the vinegar and salt. Mix and let soak for 5 minutes. Drain well.

Place the cabbage in a large bowl. Add the grated apple, onion, lemon juice, oil, and pepper. Toss lightly.

Chill for at least 1 hour before serving.

PICKLED BEETS

8 beets
1½ cups vinegar
2 teaspoons salt
¼ teaspoon freshly ground black
pepper
2 tablespoons sugar
1 onion, sliced thin
1 teaspoon caraway seeds
(optional)

Scrub the beets well. Place in a saucepan with water to cover. Bring to a boil; cover and cook for 25 minutes. Drain and cool. Peel and slice the beets.

Combine the vinegar, salt, pepper, sugar, onion, and caraway seeds in a bowl or jar. Mix well. Add the beets, basting with the liquid for a few minutes. Cover and let pickle for at least 12 hours before serving.

Serve cold.

When spring comes Jake is not far behind with a big bunch of young green vegetables because there is nothing he likes better than a Spring Salad. It makes him feel like a boy again, he says. Sammy is a boy, so it doesn't make him feel like anything, only hungry. Rosie loves it, too, because to her it means school is almost over for the year. David likes Spring Salad just because he likes vegetables in any form whatsoever. I like it because besides tasting so tasty it's easy to make.

SPRING SALAD

VEGETABLES WITH
SOUR CREAM

2 cucumbers, peeled and cubed
2 tomatoes, cubed
3 scallions (green onions), sliced
6 radishes, sliced
¾ pound cottage cheese
1½ teaspoons salt
¼ teaspoon freshly ground black
   pepper
1 pint sour cream

Combine the cucumbers, tomatoes, scallions, radishes, cottage cheese, salt, and pepper in a bowl. Mix well. Divide into 6 mounds and serve on lettuce leaves with the sour cream on top.

If desired, place the mixed vegetables in 6 individual bowls or soup plates. Fill the plates with sour cream. If prepared in this fashion, more sour cream will be required.

CUCUMBERS WITH SOUR CREAM

> 2 teaspoons salt
> 3 cucumbers, peeled and sliced
>   very thin
> 1 cup sour cream
> 3 tablespoons cider vinegar
> ⅛ teaspoon white pepper
> 1 teaspoon sugar
> 2 teaspoons chopped dill

Sprinkle the salt on the cucumbers and set aside for 30 minutes, turning them a few times. Drain thoroughly.

Mix together very well the sour cream, vinegar, pepper, sugar, and dill. Pour over the cucumbers. Chill for 1 hour.

Serve as a relish.

PICKLED CUCUMBER SALAD

> 1 cup boiling water
> 4 cucumbers, peeled and sliced
> 3 scallions (green onions), sliced,
>   or 1 onion, sliced
> 1½ teaspoons salt
> ¼ teaspoon white pepper
> 1 teaspoon sugar
> ¾ cup cider vinegar

Pour the boiling water over the cucumbers. Soak for 5 minutes. Drain well.

Combine the cucumbers with the scallions and mix. Mix the salt, pepper, sugar, and vinegar together. Pour over the cucumbers. Chill for 1 hour before serving.

Serve as a salad or relish.

POTATO SALAD

> 3 pounds small potatoes
> 2 teaspoons salt
> ½ teaspoon freshly ground black pepper
> 1 onion, finely chopped
> 2 tablespoons chopped green pepper
> 2 egg yolks
> ⅓ cup vinegar
> ½ cup olive oil

Scrub the potatoes. Place in a saucepan with water to cover. Boil for 20 minutes, or until barely tender. Drain and peel. Slice the potatoes. Add the salt, pepper, chopped onion, and green pepper. Toss lightly.

Beat the egg yolks and vinegar together. Add the olive oil very slowly, beating constantly. Pour over the potatoes. Mix well.

Serve warm or cold.

What could be better than Homemade Sauerkraut? It tastes wonderful, it's easy to make, and my family loves it, so what choice do I have? Besides, I like it too. I like it because when my mind is occupied and I don't know what to make, from the sauerkraut I can always whip up a strudel, a soup, or just have it plain with meat. It's a friend in need and tasty into the bargain. Who could ask for more?

HOMEMADE SAUERKRAUT

6 pounds cabbage
5 tablespoons salt
2 teaspoons caraway seeds
  (optional)

Cut cabbage into quarters, discarding the large outside leaves. Shred very fine. Add the salt, mixing thoroughly by hand.

Pack into sterile glass jars or a stone crock. Add the caraway seeds, if desired. Fill with cold water. Cover the jars as tightly as possible. Store in a cool, dark place for about 4 weeks.

Sometimes from tears comes a good thing. I know when I was a child I never liked to see my mother make horseradish because she would cry. It has that effect. In my own times when Rosie was a baby, she would always cry with me when I made horseradish. I could never explain to her

*that it wasn't me that was crying but the eyes, and only when
she grew up could she understand that a few tears are worth
this horseradish.*

BEET HORSERADISH

½ pound horseradish root
1 beet, grated
½ teaspoon salt
½ teaspoon sugar
4 tablespoons cider vinegar

Peel and grate the horseradish. Add the beet, salt, sugar, and vinegar.
Mix until very smooth. Store in a tightly covered glass jar.

Horseradish prepared in this fashion will keep for several weeks
in the refrigerator.

BEET-HORSERADISH SALAD

6 tablespoons prepared horseradish
3 tablespoons salad oil
1 teaspoon salt
2 teaspoons sugar
3 cups cooked, grated beets

Mix the horseradish, salad oil, salt, and sugar together. Add to the
beets, mixing lightly. Chill.

This is a delicious relish and should be served with boiled beef or
chicken.

This recipe is from my oldest living relative. Except for my mind, she is the closest link to the past. This recipe is one of her favorites for a reason that really isn't food. Like she says, in the stores you can buy Kosher Dill Pickles, but what you can't buy is the wonderful aroma that comes when you make them at home. When she first told me about why she makes her own pickles I said she was a foolish woman, but when I made them at home and Jake and David walked into the kitchen, do you believe it, it brought back such memories that we talked all night long about the old days. A very sentimental food—Kosher Dill Pickles.

KOSHER DILL PICKLES
TANTE ELKA

36 small firm cucumbers
6 tablespoons salt
12 cloves garlic
2 teaspoons pickling spice
12 sprigs dill

Scrub the cucumbers. Pack them in an upright position into glass jars. Divide the salt, garlic, pickling spice, and dill among the jars. Fill each jar to overflowing with water. Seal the jars.

Store in a dark cool place for at least 10 days before using. Chill before serving.

David likes salami, My Jake likes frankfurters, Sammy enjoys meat, Rosie's favorite is pickles, and I like potato salad. I want to serve them what they like, so for Sunday-night supper I put together everybody's likes and behold! Salad!

MIXED-UP SUNDAY-NIGHT SALAD

4 potatoes, cooked, peeled, and
  diced
4 frankfurters, cooked and sliced
  ½ inch thick
4 slices salami, cut in thin strips
2 cups diced cooked beef,
  chicken, or turkey
2 hard-cooked eggs, chopped
1 onion, sliced thin
2 dill pickles, diced
1½ teaspoons salt
½ teaspoon freshly ground black
  pepper
½ cup mayonnaise
¼ cup vinegar
¼ cup salad oil

Mix together the potatoes, frankfurters, salami, meat, eggs, onion, pickles, salt, and pepper.

Beat the mayonnaise, vinegar, and oil until smooth. Pour over the salad. Chill for 2 hours.

Serve on lettuce.

TOMATO-DILL SALAD

6 tomatoes, sliced ½ inch thick
2 onions, sliced thin
1½ teaspoons salt
2 teaspoons sugar
½ teaspoon freshly ground black
  pepper
4 tablespoons chopped dill
1 teaspoon celery seed
2 tablespoons lemon juice

In a serving dish or on individual salad plates arrange layers of the tomatoes and onions. Sprinkle with the salt, sugar, pepper, dill, celery seed, and lemon juice.

Cover and chill for at least 2 hours before serving.

BEET RING

1½ tablespoons gelatin
1 cup cold water
1 cup tomato juice
1 teaspoon grated lemon rind
2 tablespoons lemon juice
1 teaspoon salt
½ teaspoon freshly grated black
  pepper
1 cup diced cucumbers
1½ cups diced cooked beets

Soften the gelatin in ¼ cup cold water for 5 minutes. Combine remaining water, tomato juice, lemon rind, lemon juice, salt, and pepper in a saucepan. Bring to a boil; remove from heat and add gelatin, stirring until dissolved.

Place the cucumbers and beets in a lightly oiled ring mold. Pour the gelatin over the vegetables.

Chill until firm; carefully unmold. Fill the center with coleslaw or potato salad, if desired.

BEET RELISH

8 beets, peeled and chopped
  coarsely
2 onions, chopped
2 green or red peppers, chopped
3 cups chopped cabbage
2 cups vinegar
1½ tablespoons salt
½ cup sugar
3 tablespoons mustard seed
1 tablespoon celery seed

Combine the beets, onions, peppers, cabbage, vinegar, salt, sugar, mustard seed, and celery seed in a saucepan. Bring to a boil and cook 10 minutes. Pour into quart jars (about three) and seal at once.

Refrigerate for at least 48 hours before using.

PICKLED MUSHROOMS

6 tablespoons olive oil
2½ pounds mushrooms, stems
  removed
2 cups vinegar
2 teaspoons salt
12 peppercorns
4 cloves

Heat 3 tablespoons olive oil in a skillet; sauté the whole mushroom caps in it for 5 minutes. (Use the stems for soup.) Cool and place in a quart jar.

Combine the vinegar, salt, peppercorns, cloves, and remaining oil in a saucepan. Bring to a boil and cook over low heat for 10 minutes. Pour over the mushrooms.

Seal the jar and refrigerate for 3 days before using.

WALNUT-CRANBERRY RELISH

2 oranges
1 apple
1 pound cranberries
1¾ cups sugar
1 cup shelled walnuts, coarsely
    chopped

Peel the oranges and reserve half the peel. Remove the membranes and seeds of the oranges. Quarter the apple; remove the seeds and fibers. Grind the cranberries, oranges, reserved peel, and apple in a food chopper. Add the sugar and nuts; mix well.

Chill for 3 hours before serving. The relish will keep well if stored in a tightly covered container in the refrigerator.

TOMATO-PICKLE RELISH

2 pounds tomatoes, chopped and
    drained
3 cucumbers, peeled and chopped
1 green pepper, chopped
2 cups grated cabbage
1 onion, chopped
1 cup vinegar
2 cups sugar
1½ teaspoons salt
2 tablespoons mustard seed

Combine the tomatoes, cucumbers, green pepper, cabbage, onion, vinegar, sugar, salt, and mustard seed. Mix well.

Pack into sterile quart jars (about three). Seal well. Store in the refrigerator for 3 days before using. The relish will keep well.

Noodles, Breads & Pancakes

About calories we wouldn't talk. About taste, yes, but calories, no! Most of these recipes come from Katy. She married Pincus, who owns Pincus Pines, a hotel in the heart of Rip Van Winkle's country, the Catskill Mountains. Katy is a cook, but what a cook, and without her would Pincus have a hotel? People come from miles around for Katy's cooking, but her speciality is in the noodle, bread, and pancake department. She's thin like a rail too. Every summer when we take our vacation at the Pines, Katy teaches me a few new recipes and I am passing them on to you. Learning to cook them was no hardship and eating them afterward was also no trouble. It was more like a labor of love if I may say as one who shouldn't, and I think you'll find it that way too.

MALAI

CORN MEAL AND
CHEESE PUDDING

1 cake or package yeast
½ cup lukewarm water
⅓ cup sifted flour
2 cups yellow corn meal
2 teaspoons salt
1 teaspoon sugar
3 cups cold water
½ pound pot cheese, drained
6 scallions (green onions), sliced
¼ teaspoon freshly ground black
    pepper
3 tablespoons melted butter

Soak the yeast in the water for 5 minutes. Add the flour and mix well. Cover and set aside in a warm place for 1 hour.

Add the corn meal, ½ teaspoon of the salt, the sugar, and cold water, mixing very well. The batter should be the consistency of heavy cream. Preheat oven to 350°.

Pour half the batter into a buttered 2-quart casserole or baking dish. Cover with the cheese and scallions. Sprinkle with the pepper and remaining salt. Pour remaining batter over it. Pour melted butter on top.

Bake for 45 minutes, or until browned on top and firm.

Serve as an accompaniment to fish dishes or as the main part of a dairy meal.

MY FAVORITE FRENCH TOAST

¼ cup sifted flour
½ teaspoon salt
2 eggs
1 cup milk
1 teaspoon vanilla extract
6 1-inch-thick slices white bread,
    trimmed
4 tablespoons butter

Sift the flour and salt into a bowl. Beat the eggs, milk, and vanilla together and add to the flour. Beat well. Dip the bread slices into the mixture, soaking them well.

Melt the butter in a skillet. Fry the bread in it until browned on both sides.

Serve with jelly or sprinkle with sugar.

MAMALIGA

RUMANIAN CORN MEAL

2 cups yellow corn meal
1 cup cold water
2 teaspoons salt
3 cups boiling water
¼ pound butter
2 cups cottage cheese, drained

Mix the corn meal and cold water until smooth. Add the salt to the boiling water. Add the corn meal very gradually, stirring constantly to prevent lumps from forming. Cook over low heat for 30 minutes. Stir frequently. Add the butter and cottage cheese. Mix lightly and serve hot.

Serve *mamaliga* with fish dishes in place of potatoes, or as a separate course.

Blintzes! *What can I say? If I told you that my life was wrapped up in a* blintze *would you believe me? Some people have family crests, lions, tigers, unicorns, elephants—a whole menagerie—and if my family had a crest, you know what would be on it? A* blintze. *I mean it. All the good things in my life are measured in* blintzes *because by us it's not a party if there isn't a* blintze, *and who ever heard of a sad party?*

BLINTZES

THIN PANCAKES

2 eggs
2 tablespoons salad oil
1 cup milk
¾ cup sifted flour
½ teaspoon salt
6 tablespoons butter

Beat the eggs, oil, and milk together in a bowl. Add the flour and salt; beat until very smooth. Chill for 30 minutes. The batter should be the consistency of heavy cream. If the mixture is too thick, add a little milk.

Melt 1 teaspoon of the butter in a 7-inch skillet. Pour 1 tablespoon of the batter into it, turning the pan quickly so batter will cover the bottom. Fry until lightly browned on one side only. Stack the *blintzes,* browned side up, until all the batter is used, adding additional butter as required.

Place 1 tablespoon of any of the following mixtures on each of the *blintzes.* Turn two opposite sides in a little bit, and then roll up carefully. Melt the remaining butter in a large skillet. Fry the *blintzes* in it until lightly browned on both sides.

Serve hot with sour cream and a little sugar, if desired. These *blintzes* are delicious when served cold, too.

VEGETABLE FILLING
FOR BLINTZES

4 tablespoons butter
2 onions, chopped
1 green pepper, sliced thin
2 stalks celery, sliced thin
½ cup shredded cabbage
1½ teaspoons salt
¼ teaspoon pepper
2 tablespoons chopped parsley

Melt the butter in a skillet. Add the onions, green pepper, celery, cabbage, salt, and pepper. Sauté for 10 minutes, stirring frequently. Add the parsley and stir. Correct seasoning.

Cool. Proceed as directed for *blintzes*.

APPLE FILLING
FOR BLINTZES

3 apples, peeled and sliced
4 tablespoons brown sugar
½ teaspoon cinnamon
⅓ cup melted butter
⅓ cup sugar
4 tablespoons bread crumbs

Combine the apples, brown sugar, and cinnamon in a saucepan. Cook over low heat for 10 minutes, stirring frequently. Cool for 30 minutes. Fill the pancakes as directed for *blintzes*.

Place in a buttered baking dish. Sprinkle with the melted butter, sugar, and bread crumbs.

Bake in a 375° oven for 20 minutes, or until browned.

CHEESE FILLING
FOR BLINTZES

¼ pound cream cheese
¼ pound cottage cheese
2 egg yolks
2 tablespoons sugar
1 teaspoon vanilla extract

Beat the cream cheese, cottage cheese, egg yolks, sugar, and vanilla until smooth. Proceed as directed for *blintzes.*

These blintzes *are called hurry-up because they can be made very fast. I find them a big help when Jake brings his partner Mendel home to the house. I have to have something easy and fast because between Jake and Mendel there's always an argument. I know when I see them come in the door that it won't be long before Mendel will be going out the same way. I suppose that's how it is when people are partners. I don't want Mendel to go away on an empty stomach, so I make these hurry-up* blintzes.

HURRY-UP CHEESE BLINTZES

½ pound cream cheese
2 teaspoons salt
3 eggs, beaten
24 soda crackers (about 3 inches
   square)
½ cup milk
6 tablespoons butter

Beat the cheese until smooth. Add 1 teaspoon of the salt and 4 tablespoons of the beaten egg. Mix well together. Spread the mixture on 12 biscuits. Cover with the remaining 12 biscuits and press down firmly. Beat the milk, remaining salt and eggs together. Dip the sandwiches into it, soaking them well.

Melt half the butter in a skillet. Fry the sandwiches in it until lightly browned on both sides, adding more butter as necessary.

Serve hot with jelly or sugar.

Kreplach you put in soup, I put in soup, everybody puts in soup. It was a big surprise to me when I found out that kreplach is almost as international as people. In a Chinese restaurant I found it also in soup. Won Ton is the Chinese name, and how it got all the way to China is a mystery for the history books, not me. All I know is that the recipe is the same, and in good chicken soup you don't need a passport to enjoy it.

MEAT KREPLACH

1¾ cups sifted flour
1½ teaspoons salt
2 eggs
3 tablespoons shortening
½ pound ground beef
1 onion, grated
½ teaspoon freshly ground black pepper
2 tablespoons parsley

Sift the flour and ½ teaspoon of the salt onto a board. Make a well in the center and place the eggs in it. Work in the flour until a dough is formed. Knead until smooth and elastic. Roll out as thin as possible. Cut into 3-inch squares.

Melt the shortening in a skillet. Add the beef, onion, pepper, parsley, and remaining salt. Sauté for 10 minutes, stirring frequently. Let cool for 15 minutes.

Place 1 tablespoon of the beef mixture on each square. Fold the dough over the filling to form a triangle. Press the edges together firmly.

Drop into boiling water or soup. Cook for 20 minutes. If cooked in water, drain well and serve with meat dishes. If cooked in soup, serve several in each portion of soup.

KREPLACH DOUGH

STUFFED DUMPLING

2 cups sifted flour
¼ teaspoon salt
2 eggs
2 tablespoons cold water
½ cup melted butter
1 cup sour cream

Sift the flour and salt onto a board. Make a well in the center. Place the eggs and water in it. Work in the flour until a dough is formed. Knead until smooth and elastic. Cover and set aside while preparing the filling.

Roll the dough as thin as possible on a lightly floured surface. Cut into 2-inch squares. Place a heaping teaspoonful of any desired mixture on each square. Fold the dough over the filling to form a triangle, and seal the edges well.

Drop into boiling salted water. Cook for 15 minutes. Drain well.

Serve with the melted butter and sour cream. If desired, the *kreplach* may be fried after they are boiled.

PRUNE FILLING
FOR KREPLACH

1 pound unsweetened prunes,
   presoaked
⅓ cup sugar
½ cup water
½ cup orange juice
2 teaspoons lemon juice
1 tablespoon grated orange rind

Combine the prunes, sugar, water, orange juice, and lemon juice in a saucepan. Cook over medium heat for 20 minutes, or until prunes are soft. Drain and cool. Remove pits. Chop the prunes coarsely. Add the orange rind and mix.

Fill and cook the *kreplach* as directed for *kreplach* dough.

Serve with browned bread crumbs and melted butter if desired.

POTATO AND CHEESE FILLING
FOR KREPLACH

3 tablespoons butter
2 onions, chopped
2 cups mashed potatoes
1 cup cottage cheese, drained
1 egg
1½ teaspoons salt
¼ teaspoon freshly ground black
   pepper

Melt the butter in a skillet. Sauté the onions in it for 15 minutes, stirring frequently.

Beat together the potatoes, cottage cheese, egg, salt, pepper, and onions until smooth.

Proceed as directed for *kreplach* dough.

182

CHEESE FILLING
FOR KREPLACH

1 pound cottage cheese, drained
2 egg yolks
¾ teaspoon salt

Mix the cheese, egg yolks, and salt together until very well blended. Proceed as directed for *kreplach* dough.

KASHA KREPLACH (BUCKWHEAT GROATS)

FILLED POCKETS
OF DOUGH

2 cups sifted flour
1½ teaspoons salt
3 eggs
2 tablespoons cold water
3 tablespoons shortening
1½ cups cooked *kasha*
 (*see page 207*)
1½ cups grated onion
¼ teaspoon freshly ground black
 pepper

Sift the flour and ½ teaspoon of the salt onto a board. Make a well in the center. Place 2 of the eggs and the water in it. Work in the flour gradually, kneading until a dough is formed. Knead until smooth and elastic. Cover and set aside while preparing the filling.

Melt the shortening in a skillet. Add the *kasha*, onion, pepper, and remaining salt. Sauté for 5 minutes, stirring occasionally. Let cool for 15 minutes. Add the remaining egg and mix well.

Roll out the dough as thin as possible on a lightly floured surface. Cut into 3-inch squares. Place 1 tablespoon of the mixture on each. Fold the dough over the filling to form a triangle, sealing the edges well.

Drop into boiling salted water. Cook for 15 minutes, or until they rise to the surface. Drain well. Do not cook too many at one time. Serve in soup or as an accompaniment to a meat course. If desired, drain well and brown the *kreplach* in a skillet with a little shortening.

MUSHROOM FILLING FOR KREPLACH

2 tablespoons shortening
1 onion, chopped
1 pound mushrooms, chopped
1 teaspoon salt
¼ teaspoon freshly ground black pepper
2 egg yolks, beaten

Melt the shortening in a skillet. Add the onion and sauté for 5 minutes, stirring frequently. Add the mushrooms. Sauté 10 minutes, or until the mixture is dry, stirring occasionally. Add salt and pepper. Cool for 15 minutes. Add the egg yolks and mix well. Cool for 30 minutes additional.

Fill and cook the *kreplach* as directed for *kreplach* dough.

These *kreplach* are delicious as an accompaniment to meat or fish dishes.

Who is Sylvia? She's Tante Elka's middle boy Georgie's wife. When she and Georgie got married it looked like she was going to be a regular daughter-in-law. But she turned out fine. How? Knishes. That was the turning point. Elka thought Sylvia was stuck-up and she was very worried that it would be contagious to Georgie, but one afternoon Elka fell into Sylvia's apartment and found her making knishes, *so everything was all right from that moment on. Like Elka says:* "You couldn't be stuck-up and make knishes too." *And that's the truth. Show me someone who can make* knishes *and I'll show you a person. No matter what they call them or how they serve them, a* knish *is a* knish *and that's all.*

CHEESE KNISHES (PASTRIES)

2 cups sifted flour
2 teaspoons baking powder
1½ teaspoons salt
⅓ pound butter
1 egg, beaten
½ cup milk
6 scallions (green onions), sliced,
    or 2 onions, chopped
½ pound cottage cheese, drained
4 tablespoons sour cream
1 egg yolk

Sift the flour, baking powder, and ½ teaspoon of the salt into a bowl. Cut in ¼ pound of the butter with a pastry blender or 2 knives. Combine the egg and milk and add, tossing lightly until a ball of dough is formed. Chill for 1 hour.

Melt the remaining butter in a skillet. Sauté the scallions in it for 5 minutes, stirring frequently. Beat the cottage cheese, sour cream, egg yolk, and remaining salt until smooth. Add the scallions and mix together well. Preheat oven to 350°.

Roll out the dough ⅛ inch thick on a lightly floured surface. Cut into 3-inch circles. Place 1 tablespoon of the cheese mixture on each. Fold the dough over the mixture and pinch the edges together. Place on a buttered cooky sheet, solid side down.

Bake for 30 minutes, or until browned. Serve hot or cold, with sour cream, if desired.

POTATO KNISHES (PASTRIES)

6 tablespoons shortening
2 onions, chopped
4 cups mashed potatoes
3 eggs
¾ cup sifted flour
1 teaspoon salt
⅛ teaspoon white pepper
2 tablespoons grated onion

Melt 4 tablespoons of the shortening in a skillet. Add the chopped onions. Sauté for 10 minutes, stirring frequently. Remove the onions and cool. Preheat oven to 375°.

Melt the remaining shortening in the skillet. Mix together the potatoes, eggs, flour, salt, pepper, grated onion, and melted shortening. Knead until smooth. Break off pieces and shape into 2-inch balls. Make a depression in the center of each, and fill with a teaspoonful of the sautéed onions. Cover the filling with the dough. Flatten the balls slightly with the palm. Place on a greased baking sheet.

Bake in a 375° oven for 25 minutes, or until browned.

Chopped liver may be substituted for the onions, if desired.

PIEROGEN
(FILLED PASTRY)

1½ cups sifted flour
½ teaspoon salt
½ teaspoon baking powder
½ cup shortening
1 egg, beaten
2 tablespoons cold water

Sift the flour, salt, and baking powder into a bowl. Cut in the shortening with a pastry blender or 2 knives. Add the egg and cold water, tossing lightly until a ball of dough is formed. Chill while preparing the filling.

Preheat oven to 375°. Roll the dough ⅛ inch thick on a lightly floured surface. Cut into 3-inch circles. Place a tablespoon of any desired mixture on each. Fold the dough over the filling, sealing the edges well.

Place on a greased baking sheet. Bake for 20 minutes, or until browned.

Serve as an accompaniment to meat dishes. A very small version makes a good *hors d'oeuvre*.

MUSHROOM FILLING FOR PIEROGEN

3 tablespoons shortening
1 pound mushrooms, chopped
2 onions, chopped
2 tablespoons chopped parsley
1 tablespoon chopped dill
   (optional)
2 hard-cooked egg yolks, mashed
1½ teaspoons salt
¼ teaspoon freshly ground black
   pepper
½ cup bread crumbs
2 tablespoons sour cream
   (optional)

Melt the shortening in a skillet. Add the mushrooms and onions. Sauté for 10 minutes, or until all the mushroom liquid is evaporated. Add the parsley, dill, egg yolks, salt, pepper, bread crumbs, and sour cream. Mix well.

Proceed as directed for *pierogen*.

POTATO FILLING
FOR PIEROGEN

¼ cup shortening
2 onions chopped
2 tablespoons chopped parsley
1½ cups mashed, cooked
    potatoes
1 egg yolk
¼ teaspoon freshly ground black
    pepper
1 teaspoon salt

Melt the shortening in a skillet. Sauté the onions in it for 10 minutes, stirring frequently. Add the parsley and potatoes. Cook over low heat for 5 minutes, stirring constantly. Remove from heat and let cool for 10 minutes. Add the egg yolk, pepper, and salt. Mix.

Proceed as directed for *pierogen*.

PIROSHKI

STUFFED PASTRIES

2 cups sifted flour
½ teaspoon baking powder
½ teaspoon salt
¾ cup shortening
1 egg, beaten
3 tablespoons cold water

Sift the flour, baking powder, and salt into a bowl. Cut in the shortening with a pastry blender or 2 knives. Mix the egg and water together and add, tossing lightly until a ball of dough is formed. Chill for 1 hour.

Roll dough ⅛ inch thick on a lightly floured board. Cut into 3-inch circles. Place a tablespoon of any of the following mixtures on it. Fold the dough over the filling, sealing the edges carefully. Place on a well-greased baking sheet.

Bake in a 375° oven for 20 minutes. Serve hot with *borscht* or hot consommé. They also make excellent *hors d'oeuvres*.

POTATO FILLING FOR PIROSHKI

6 tablespoons shortening
4 onions, chopped
2 cups mashed potatoes
1 teaspoon salt
¼ teaspoon freshly ground black
  pepper

Melt the shortening in a skillet. Sauté the onions in it for 15 minutes, stirring frequently. Add the potatoes, salt, and pepper. Mix lightly. Cool for 15 minutes and proceed as directed for *piroshki*.

LIVER AND MUSHROOM FILLING FOR PIROSHKI

4 tablespoons shortening
1 onion, chopped
½ pound mushrooms, chopped
¼ pound chicken livers, chopped
1½ teaspoons salt
¼ teaspoon freshly ground black
  pepper

Melt half of the shortening in a skillet. Add the onion and mushrooms. Sauté for 15 minutes, stirring frequently. Remove and set aside.

Melt the remaining shortening in the skillet. Sauté the livers in it for 10 minutes. Add to the mushroom mixture along with the salt and pepper. Chop until very smooth. Correct seasoning. Let cool for 5 minutes, and proceed as directed for *piroshki*.

The Molly Goldberg Cookbook

FISH FILLING FOR PIROSHKI

> 3 tablespoons butter
> 1 onion, chopped
> ½ pound fish fillet
> 2 hard-cooked egg yolks
> 2 tablespoons chopped parsley
> 1½ teaspoons salt
> ¼ teaspoon freshly ground black
>   pepper
> 2 tablespoons sour cream

Melt the butter in a skillet. Add the onion and fish. Sauté for 15 minutes, stirring occasionally. Chop the onion, fish, and egg yolks together. Add the parsley, salt, pepper, and sour cream. Mix well. Proceed as directed for _piroshki_.

To think that just a few short years ago there were only a few weeks in the summer that you could make these cherry verenikas because the cherries were only in season for such a short time. But today you can have them any time you want because of the frozen and canned cherries you can buy anyplace. My Uncle David is still amazed when we have them in the winter. It's hard for him to get used to the idea, but he eats them just the same. The mind and the appetite are birds of a different color, I guess. Today there is no season for these verenikas, only when the mood strikes you.

CHERRY VERENIKAS

CHERRY DUMPLINGS

3 cups sour red cherries, fresh, frozen, or canned
1 cup sugar
1 tablespoon lemon juice
1 tablespoon cornstarch
2 cups sifted flour
½ teaspoon salt
2 eggs
3 tablespoons water
½ cup sour cream

Pit the cherries. Combine in a saucepan with the juice from the cherries, the sugar, lemon juice, and cornstarch. Mix well. Cook over low heat for 5 minutes, stirring occasionally. Remove the cherries, reserving the juice. If the juice is not syrupy, cook over low heat until it thickens. Let the cherries cool while preparing the dough.

Sift the flour and salt onto a board. Make a well in the center. Place the eggs and water in it. Work in the flour gradually, mixing until a dough is formed. Knead until smooth.

Roll the dough as thin as possible on a lightly floured board. Cut into 3- or 4-inch rounds. Place a few cherries in each. Fold the dough over the cherries, sealing the edges very carefully.

Drop into boiling, lightly salted water. Boil for 10 minutes, or until they rise to the surface. Drain well. Do not cook too many at once.

Serve warm with the syrup and sour cream.

NOTE: Blueberries or huckleberries may be substituted for the cherries.

Bagels *is a roll. It's more of a varnished doughnut made with a special bread dough. It is a thing of beauty to behold, especially on a cold Sunday morning in the winter. The bagel is a lonely roll to eat all by yourself because in order for the true taste to come out you need your family. One to cut the bagels, one to toast them, one to put on the cream cheese and the lox, one to put them on the table, and one to supervise. That's My Jake. He supervises and the bagel wouldn't taste the same without him, so that's why these are called* Bagels Jake. *Lox, in case you didn't know, is like smoked Nova Scotia salmon, only saltier.*

BAGELS JAKE

1 cake or package yeast
2 tablespoons sugar
⅔ cup lukewarm water
3 tablespoons melted shortening
3 cups sifted flour
1 teaspoon salt
1 egg

Dissolve the yeast and sugar in the water. Add the shortening and mix together.

Sift the flour and salt onto a board. Make a well in the center and pour the yeast mixture and the egg into it. Work in the flour, kneading until smooth and elastic. Place the dough in a bowl; cover and let rise for 45 minutes. Knead again for 3 minutes. Divide the dough into 12 pieces. Roll between lightly floured hands into 8-inch strips. Form into doughnuts and press the edges together securely.

Place on a floured baking sheet and broil in a 400° oven for 4 minutes. Remove and drop into rapidly boiling water. Cook for 20

minutes. Drain well. Replace on the baking sheet. Bake in a 400°
oven for 15 minutes, or until browned on both sides.

To serve, slice through the middle horizontally and spread with
butter or cream cheese. *Bagels* are particularly good with smoked
salmon.

The family named this challah *recipe after me. They
insisted. They said of all the recipes this one brings to them
the sweetest memories. To me too it brings memories. Of
course, now the children are all grown up, but when they
were small and I made* challah, *I would always make enough
dough so that they could each make their own loaves. Each
year as they got older I would give them more dough to make
a bigger bread, and before you knew it they were making
loaves of* challah *as big as mine. Time flies, especially in the*
challah *department.*

CHALLAH À LA MOLLY

EGG BREAD

1 cake or package yeast
⅛ teaspoon saffron
1 cup lukewarm water
4 cups sifted flour
1 teaspoon salt
2 teaspoons sugar
2 eggs, beaten
1 egg yolk, beaten

Soak the yeast and saffron in the water for 5 minutes. Sift the flour,
salt, and sugar together. Combine the yeast mixture with 1½ cups
of the flour mixture, stirring until smooth. Cover the bowl with a
cloth and allow to rise in a warm place until double in bulk, about

30 minutes. Add the eggs and mix well. Add the remaining flour mixture and knead on a lightly floured surface until smooth and elastic. Place the dough in a bowl, dust the top with a little flour, and cover with the cloth. Allow to rise until double in bulk, about 2 hours.

Knead the dough for 3 minutes. Divide it into 3 equal parts. Roll each piece between lightly floured hands into long, round strips. Fasten the 3 strips together at one end, and braid them. Place on a greased baking sheet. Cover and allow to rise again for 1 hour.

Preheat oven to 400°. Brush the top of the *challah* with the egg yolk.

Bake in a 400° oven for 10 minutes. Reduce heat to 375° and bake for 35 minutes longer, or until delicately browned on top.

ONION KUCHEN (BREAD)

1 cup milk
¼ pound butter
1 cake or package yeast
¼ cup lukewarm water
3 cups sifted flour
1 teaspoon salt
1½ teaspoons sugar
4 onions, sliced thin
1 egg, beaten
¼ cup sour cream
2 tablespoons poppy seeds

Combine the milk and half of the butter in a saucepan. Bring to a boil, stirring until butter melts. Remove from heat and let cool for 10 minutes.

Soften the yeast in the water for 10 minutes.

Combine the yeast and milk mixtures and mix well. Sift the flour, ½ teaspoon of the salt, and the sugar together and add to the yeast mixture, mixing well. Cover and let rise in a warm place until double in bulk, about 1½ hours.

Melt the remaining butter in a skillet. Add the onions and sauté for 10 minutes, stirring frequently. Cool. Beat the egg, sour cream, and remaining salt together.

Knead the dough. Break off pieces and roll into 2-inch balls between floured hands. Place on a baking sheet and flatten slightly. Press the sautéed onions into the *kuchen*. Spread with the sour-cream mixture. Sprinkle with the poppy seeds. Let rise for 45 minutes. Preheat oven to 375°.

Bake for 25 minutes, or until browned on top.

POTATO DUMPLINGS

4 potatoes, peeled, grated, and
   drained (about 4 cups)
½ cup sifted flour
2 eggs
2 teaspoons salt
1 tablespoon grated onion
2 tablespoons matzo or cracker
   meal

Combine the potatoes, flour, eggs, salt, onion, and matzo meal. Mix well. Form into 1-inch balls. If the mixture is not firm enough, add a little more flour.

Drop into boiling salted water. Boil for 20 minutes. Drain well. Serve in soup or with meat dishes.

NOCKERL

EGG DUMPLINGS

2 eggs
⅓ cup cold water
1 teaspoon salt
⅓ cup sifted flour
½ teaspoon baking powder

Beat the eggs, water, and salt together. Add the flour and baking powder, mixing until smooth.

Drop by the teaspoonful into boiling salted water. Cook for 5 minutes, or until the *nockerl* rise to the surface. Drain well.

Serve in soup, or with *paprikas* or goulash. They may also be eaten plain with a little melted butter or other shortening.

FARFEL

EGG BARLEY

2 eggs
½ teaspoon salt
2 cups sifted flour

Beat the eggs and salt together. Add the flour gradually, adding just enough to form a stiff dough. It may not be necessary to add all the flour.

Break off pieces of the dough and roll into pencil-thin strips between floured hands. Set aside for 1 hour.

Chop the dough into small pieces about the size of barley. Let dry for several hours on a flat surface.

Drop half of the *farfel* into boiling soup and cook for 15 minutes. The remaining *farfel* may be stored in a covered jar. Serve the *farfel* in the soup.

If desired, *farfel* may be served as an accompaniment to meat dishes. Cook half of the *farfel* in boiling water for 15 minutes. Drain well and prepare in the following manner:

3 tablespoons shortening
2 onions, chopped
1 teaspoon salt
½ teaspoon freshly ground black
    pepper

Melt the shortening in a skillet. Add the onions, salt, and pepper. Sauté for 10 minutes, stirring frequently. Add the *farfel* and sauté for 5 minutes longer, stirring frequently. Serve hot with meat dishes.

This recipe comes to me from Muttle. Muttle is the family problem because everything he does he does wrong. The Pancake Noodles is the only thing he ever did right, and Jake thinks that that was a mistake too. Jake says he probably started out to poach eggs and this is what happened, but nevertheless I like to give credit where credit is due, so here is Muttle's recipe for Pancake Noodles. Jake to the contrary.

MUTTLE'S PANCAKE NOODLES

3 eggs
3 tablespoons water
1 teaspoon salt
3 tablespoons sifted potato starch
3 tablespoons matzo meal
3 tablespoons shortening

Beat the eggs, water, and salt together in a bowl. Add the potato starch and matzo meal. Mix well.

Melt half of the shortening in a 7-inch skillet. Pour 3 tablespoons of the batter into it, turning the pan quickly to coat the bottom. Fry until lightly browned on both sides. Roll up and keep warm while preparing the balance of the pancakes. Add additional shortening as necessary.

Cut into ⅛-inch strips. Serve in soups.

MANDLEN

BAKED SOUP NOODLES

2 eggs
2 teaspoons salad oil
½ teaspoon salt
1 cup sifted flour
½ teaspoon baking powder

Beat the eggs lightly. Add the salad oil and salt. Mix together. Sift the flour and baking powder together and add to the eggs, adding just enough to make a soft dough. It may not be necessary to add all of the flour mixture. Knead for a few minutes.

Break off pieces of dough and roll between floured hands in pencil-thin strips. Cut into ½-inch lengths. Preheat oven to 375°.

Place on a greased baking sheet. Bake for 12 minutes, or until lightly browned. Shake the pan frequently while baking.

Add to consommés or beef soups at the last moment before serving.

ALMOND DROPS

2 egg yolks
1 tablespoon flour or potato
  starch
1 teaspoon salt
½ cup ground blanched almonds
2 egg whites, stiffly beaten
Fat for deep frying

Beat the egg yolks in a bowl. Add the flour, salt, and almonds. Mix well. Fold in the egg whites.

Heat the fat to 375°. Drop the batter by the ½ teaspoonful into it. Fry for 2 minutes, or until browned. Drain well.

Serve in soup.

EGG DROPS

1 egg
3 tablespoons water
3 tablespoons flour
¼ teaspoon salt
2 teaspoons chopped parsley
 (optional)

Beat the egg and water together. Add the flour, salt, and parsley. Mix until smooth. Drop by the ½ teaspoonful into boiling soup. Cover and cook over medium heat for 10 minutes.

The egg drops are particularly good in beef or chicken soup.

LIVER DUMPLINGS

1 tablespoon shortening
1 onion, chopped
1 clove garlic, minced
1 pound calf's liver, skinned
1½ teaspoons salt
¼ teaspoon freshly ground black
 pepper
3 tablespoons flour
2 egg yolks
2 egg whites
½ cup melted chicken fat
3 tablespoons bread crumbs

Melt the shortening in a skillet. Sauté the onion and garlic for 5 minutes, stirring frequently.

Grind or chop the liver and sautéed onions until very smooth. Add the salt, pepper, and flour, mixing very well. Add the egg yolks and mix well.

Beat the egg whites until stiff but not dry. Fold them into the liver mixture gently.

Drop the mixture by the tablespoon into boiled, salted water. Boil for 25 minutes, or until dumplings rise to the surface. Drain well and serve with the melted chicken fat and bread crumbs.

Serve as an accompaniment to meat or poultry dishes.

FARINA DUMPLINGS

> 1 cup milk
> 2 tablespoons butter
> ½ cup farina
> 1½ teaspoons salt
> ¼ teaspoon white pepper
> 2 eggs, beaten

Combine the milk and butter in the top of a double boiler. Bring to a boil and place over hot water. Gradually add the farina, stirring constantly. Add the salt and pepper. Cook until thick, about 15 minutes, stirring occasionally. Cool for 15 minutes.

Add the eggs, mixing well. Drop by the teaspoonful into water or soup. Boil for 5 minutes. If boiled in water, drain and serve with melted butter. If boiled in soup, serve in it.

CHEESE PANCAKES

> 1 pound cottage cheese, drained
>   thoroughly
> 2 eggs
> ½ teaspoon salt
> 4 tablespoons sugar
> 2 tablespoons sour cream
> 1 cup sifted flour
> 3 tablespoons chopped seedless
>   raisins or candied fruit
>   (optional)
> 6 tablespoons butter

Force the cheese through a sieve. Add the eggs, salt, sugar, and sour cream. Beat well. Add the flour and mix well. Add the chopped fruit if desired.

Melt half the butter in a skillet. Form the cheese mixture into a pancake. Fry until lightly browned on both sides.

Serve with sour cream, sugar, and cinnamon.

Progress is a wonderful thing, and if you think that progress can't come to potato latkes you're very much mistaken. In the old days when Jake and I were first married, to make potato latkes was a long chore, but what don't you do for someone you love? So I scraped potatoes for hours. Nowadays I still love Jake but I don't work so hard and the latkes are just as good as they ever were, according to Jake. I put the potatoes in an electric mixer, and before you know it a couple of hours work is done in a minute. Progress!

POTATO LATKES (PANCAKES)

4 potatoes, peeled, grated, and drained
1 onion, grated
1 teaspoon salt
¼ teaspoon freshly ground black pepper
1 egg, beaten
3 tablespoons potato starch or flour
½ teaspoon baking powder
½ cup shortening

Mix the potatoes, onion, salt, pepper, egg, potato starch, and baking powder until very smooth.

Heat the shortening in a skillet. Drop the potato mixture into it by the tablespoonful. Fry until browned on both sides. Drain well.

Serve with meat dishes, or with applesauce as a separate course.

NOTE: The potatoes may be grated in an electric blender.

BLINI

RAISED BUCKWHEAT
PANCAKES

1 cake or package yeast
¼ cup lukewarm water
2¾ cups lukewarm milk
2 cups sifted buckwheat flour
4 egg yolks
1 tablespoon sugar
1 teaspoon salt
3 tablespoons melted butter
4 egg whites
4 tablespoons butter

Dissolve the yeast in the water. Add ¾ cup of the milk and ¾ cup of the buckwheat flour. Mix until smooth. Cover and set aside in a warm place to rise for 2 hours.

Beat the egg yolks. Add the sugar, salt, melted butter, and remaining milk and buckwheat flour. Add to the raised mixture. Mix well.

Beat the egg whites until stiff but not dry. Fold into the buckwheat mixture thoroughly.

Melt a little butter in a skillet. Drop the batter into it by the tablespoonful. Fry until browned on both sides, adding additional butter as necessary. Remove the pancakes and keep warm until all are ready.

Serve with additional melted butter and sour cream.

It's good to have a change once in a while, and something like a Noodle Layer Pudding is put down here by me in order for you to have a change. Too much of a good thing is also not good, and from time to time you might want to change over from meat and poultry. This recipe is a meal in itself, also it is good after you have fish when you make a dairy meal. Howsoever that may be, you will find this a welcome addition to the family menu no matter what. Also, this is easy to make and we often eat it when the mood overtakes us. But no matter what your desire, you will find it utterly. Yes.

NOODLE LAYER PUDDING

1 pound cottage cheese, drained
4 egg yolks
½ cup heavy cream
2 tablespoons sugar
1 teaspoon salt
1 pound broad noodles, cooked
    and drained
¼ cup bread crumbs
4 tablespoons melted butter

Force the cottage cheese through a sieve. (If an electric mixer is to be used, omit this step.)

Beat the cottage cheese, egg yolks, cream, sugar, and salt together until smooth.

In a buttered baking dish arrange alternate layers of the noodles and the cheese mixture, starting and ending with the noodles. Make as many layers as possible. Sprinkle the bread crumbs and butter on top.

Bake in a 375° oven for 30 minutes.

NOODLE-APPLE PUDDING

4 tablespoons shortening
½ pound fine noodles, cooked
　　and drained
3 eggs
¼ cup sugar
1 teaspoon cinnamon
½ cup bread crumbs
3 cups sweetened applesauce,
　　fresh or canned

Melt the shortening in a skillet. Sauté the noodles in it until browned.

Beat the eggs, sugar, cinnamon, and ¼ cup of the bread crumbs together. Add the noodles and mix well.

In a greased baking dish arrange alternate layers of the noodle mixture and the applesauce, starting and ending with the noodles. Sprinkle the remaining bread crumbs on top.

Bake in a 350° oven for 30 minutes.

NOODLES AND CHEESE

1 pound pot cheese or cottage
　　cheese
1 cup sour cream
1 pound noodles, cooked and
　　drained
1 teaspoon salt
4 scallions (green onions), sliced
　　(optional)

Beat the pot cheese and sour cream together in a saucepan. Add the noodles and salt. Toss lightly over low heat until thoroughly heated. Add the scallions, if desired.

The noodles may be baked in a 375° oven for 20 minutes if desired, instead of heating over direct heat.

NOODLES WITH MOHN (POPPY SEEDS)

1 cup milk
⅓ cup brown sugar
½ cup poppy seeds
1 pound broad noodles, cooked
and drained

Combine the milk, brown sugar, and poppy seeds in a large saucepan. Bring to a boil and cook over low heat for 5 minutes, stirring occasionally. Add the noodles. Mix lightly and heat.

Serve hot as a dessert.

KASHE VARNISHKES

NOODLES WITH BUCKWHEAT
GROATS

1 cup medium buckwheat groats
1 egg, beaten
1¾ cups boiling water
2 teaspoons salt
6 tablespoons shortening
2 onions, chopped
½ pound broad noodles, broken
in half, cooked, and drained
½ teaspoon freshly ground black
pepper

Mix the groats and egg in a saucepan over low heat until each grain is separate. Add the water and 1 teaspoon of the salt. Cover and cook over low heat for 12 minutes.

205

Melt the shortening in a skillet. Sauté the onions in it for 10 minutes, stirring frequently. Add the noodles, buckwheat groats, pepper, and remaining salt. Mix together lightly and heat before serving.

Serve with meat dishes.

KOLATCHEN

SOUR CREAM BISCUITS

1 cake or package yeast
¼ cup lukewarm water
¼ pound butter
2 eggs
3 tablespoons sugar
1 teaspoon salt
2 teaspoons grated lemon rind
1 cup sour cream
3 cups sifted flour
1 egg white, beaten

Soften the yeast in the water for 5 minutes.

Cream the butter. Add the eggs, sugar, salt, lemon rind, sour cream and yeast. Beat well. Add the flour, mixing well. Knead until smooth. Roll out 1 inch thick on a lightly floured board. Cut into 2-inch circles. Place on a buttered cooky sheet and let rise for 1 hour. Press down the center of each biscuit to form a ridge around the edges. Brush with the egg white.

Bake in a 375° oven for 20 minutes.

Serve warm.

MOHN KICHLACH

POPPY-SEED BISCUITS

1 cup sifted flour
¾ teaspoon baking powder
⅛ teaspoon salt
2 tablespoons sugar
⅓ cup poppy seeds
⅓ cup salad oil
2 eggs, beaten
1 tablespoon ice water

Sift the flour, baking powder, salt, and sugar into a bowl. Add the poppy seeds and mix. Make a well in the center. Place the oil, eggs, and water in it. Work in the flour, mixing until a heavy batter is formed. Preheat oven to 325°.

Drop the batter by the teaspoonful onto a greased cooky sheet, leaving about 2 inches between each.

Bake for 20 minutes, or until browned.

KASHA (BUCKWHEAT GROATS)

1 cup *kasha*, medium or coarse
1 egg
1 teaspoon salt
2 cups boiling water

Mix the *kasha*, egg, and salt in a saucepan. Place over low heat and cook, stirring constantly, until each grain is dry and separate. Add boiling water; cover and cook over low heat 12 to 15 minutes, or until dry and tender.

Serve as a substitute for rice or potatoes, or use as directed in recipe. This recipe makes about 3½ to 4 cups.

FRIED CHEESE SPECIAL, 3E.

12 slices white bread, trimmed
6 slices mozzarella cheese or
    white American cheese
6 anchovies, mashed
½ cup milk
½ cup bread crumbs
2 eggs
½ teaspoon salt
½ cup olive oil
½ cup salad oil

Make 6 sandwiches of the bread, cheese, and anchovies. Dip in the milk and then in the bread crumbs. Beat the eggs and salt together, and dip the sandwiches, coating them well.

Combine and heat the oils to 360°. Fry sandwiches until golden brown on both sides. Drain and serve hot.

Desserts

By some people the meal itself is a long delay between the appetizer and the dessert. The desserts in this section are from all my neighbors, and for some reason, no matter how much a person says they can't cook, they always have a favorite dessert that they can make better than anyone else. So the best desserts of my acquaintances I have here.

The sweet tooth is universal, and if the politicians would stop talking and let their wives trade dessert recipes, between the mixing and the measuring an understanding would arise and the world would have peace. "Let them eat cake," a famous lady said. I don't know whether she was a cook or not but she had the right idea, only she should have added pies and puddings and cookies, but maybe cakes was her favorite dessert.

SCHNECKEN

SNAILS

3 cups sifted flour
2 tablespoons sugar
⅛ teaspoon salt
½ pound butter
1 cake or package yeast
½ cup lukewarm milk
3 egg yolks

Sift the flour, sugar, and salt together into a bowl. Work in the butter by hand.

Soften the yeast in the milk for 5 minutes in a bowl. Add the egg yolks. Beat with a rotary beater for 3 minutes. Add to the flour mixture, mixing until a dough is formed. Wrap in wax paper and chill overnight in the refrigerator. Remove from the refrigerator ½ hour before it is to be used, and prepare the filling:

2 cups ground walnuts
1 cup sugar
1 tablespoon cinnamon
1 egg, beaten
2 egg whites, stiffly beaten

Mix the walnuts, sugar, cinnamon, and egg together. Roll out the dough ⅛ inch thick on a lightly floured surface. Spread the egg whites over it, and then the walnut mixture. Roll up carefully, as for a jelly roll. Cut into ½-inch slices and place on a buttered baking sheet.

Let rise in a warm place for 30 minutes.
Preheat oven to 425°. Bake for 20 minutes, or until browned.

HAZELNUT ROLL

1 cake or package yeast
2 tablespoons lukewarm water
⅓ cup scalded milk, cooled
¼ pound butter
¾ cup sugar
4 egg yolks
2 cups sifted flour
½ teaspoon salt
2 teaspoons vanilla extract
2 cups ground hazelnuts
  (filberts)
¼ cup light cream
1 egg white

Soften the yeast in the water for 5 minutes. Add the milk and mix well.

Cream the butter. Add ¼ cup sugar and beat well. Add 1 egg yolk at a time, beating well after each addition. Add the flour and salt and mix again. Add the yeast mixture and 1 teaspoon of the vanilla. Beat until smooth. Cover and set aside until double in bulk, about 2 hours.

Mix the nuts and remaining sugar. Add the cream and remaining vanilla. Mix well.

Punch down the dough. Roll out on a lightly floured surface until about ¼ inch thick. Spread the nut mixture over it. Roll up as for a jelly roll. Place on a buttered baking sheet and brush with the egg white. Let rise for 1 hour. Preheat oven to 375°.

Bake for 25 minutes, or until browned.

NOTE: Other nuts may be substituted for the hazelnuts.

POLISH PRUNE CAKE

2 pounds prunes
1¼ cups sugar
1 cake or package yeast
¼ cup lukewarm water
¼ cup light cream, scalded and
    cooled
2¼ cups sifted flour
½ teaspoon salt
¼ pound butter, melted
2 egg yolks
½ pint heavy cream
2 tablespoons cinnamon

Soak the prunes in water to cover overnight. Drain and pit.

Soften 1 tablespoon of the sugar and the yeast in the water for 5 minutes. Add the cream and 1 cup of the flour. Mix well. Cover and allow to rise in a warm place for 1½ hours. Add the remaining flour, the salt, half of the melted butter, the egg yolks, and ½ cup of the sugar. Knead until smooth. Cover and set aside for 2 hours, or until double in bulk.

Roll out the dough ½ inch thick on a lightly floured board. Line a deep baking pan, about 8 x 12 inches, with the dough. Cover and let rise for 30 minutes.

Preheat oven to 350°. Brush the dough with the remaining butter. Arrange the prunes on the dough in even rows. Pour the cream over them. Mix the cinnamon and remaining sugar and sprinkle on top.

Bake for 35 minutes. Cut into squares and serve warm or cold.

CINNAMON CAKE

4 tablespoons butter
1¼ cups sugar
1 egg
1¼ cups sifted flour
1 teaspoon cream of tartar
½ teaspoon baking soda
¼ teaspoon salt
½ cup milk
4 tablespoons cinnamon

Cream the butter. Add 1 cup of the sugar. Beat until thick and light in color. Add the egg, beating well. Preheat oven to 350°.

Sift together the flour, cream of tartar, baking soda, and salt. Add to the butter mixture alternately with the milk. Mix well.

Pour the mixture into a buttered 8-inch square pan. Mix the cinnamon and remaining sugar together and sprinkle on top.

Bake for 25 minutes, or until a cake tester comes out clean.

Cut into squares and serve warm.

STREUSELKUCHEN

CRUMB CAKE

1 cake or package yeast
¼ cup lukewarm water
¼ cup lukewarm light cream
2 cups sifted flour
4 tablespoons butter
⅓ cup sugar
2 eggs
⅛ teaspoon salt
2 tablespoons melted butter

Soften the yeast in the water for 5 minutes. Add the cream, stirring until smooth. Add ½ cup flour; mix well. Cover and let rise in a warm place for 1 hour.

Cream the butter; add the sugar, eggs, and salt. Beat well. Add the remaining flour and the yeast mixture. Knead until smooth and elastic. Pat into an 8-inch-square baking pan. Brush with melted butter. Let rise for 30 minutes. Preheat oven to 350°. Now prepare the crumbs:

> 3 tablespoons butter
> 2 tablespoons sugar
> 1 cup sifted flour
> 1 teaspoon cinnamon

Melt the butter; add the sugar, flour, and cinnamon, mixing well. Crumble over the cake.

Bake 30 minutes, or until browned on top. Cut into squares and serve warm or cold.

APPLE SCHALETH (CHARLOTTE)

> 2 cups sifted flour
> ½ teaspoon salt
> 3 eggs
> 2 egg yolks
> 2 tablespoons cold water
> 6 apples, peeled and sliced
> ¼ cup sugar
> ¼ cup seedless raisins
> ⅛ teaspoon nutmeg
> 3 tablespoons Malaga wine

Sift the flour and salt onto a board. Make a well in the center. Place the eggs, egg yolks, and water in it. Work in the flour, kneading until smooth and elastic. Set aside for 15 minutes.

Combine the apples and sugar in a saucepan. Cook over low heat for 10 minutes, stirring frequently. Add the raisins, nutmeg, and Malaga wine. Mix well. Preheat oven to 350°.

Divide the dough in half. Roll out as thin as possible on a floured surface. Line a 9-inch greased pie plate with it. Fill with the apple mixture and cover with the remaining half of the dough, which should also be rolled as thin as possible. Seal the edges well. Make a few slits across the top of the dough and brush with a beaten egg if desired.

Bake for 50 minutes. Let cool for 10 minutes and serve warm.

YEAST APPLE ROLL

> 4 tablespoons butter
> ½ cup milk
> ¾ cup sugar
> 1 cake or package yeast
> 1 teaspoon vanilla extract
> ½ teaspoon mace
> ½ teaspoon salt
> 2 eggs
> 2½ cups sifted flour
> 3 apples, peeled and sliced
> 1 teaspoon cinnamon
> 3 tablespoons bread crumbs
> 4 tablespoons confectioners'
>   sugar

Combine the butter, ¼ cup of the milk, and ½ cup of the sugar in a saucepan. Heat until the sugar dissolves. Let cool.

Dissolve the yeast in the remaining milk. Beat the vanilla, mace, salt, and eggs in a bowl. Add the yeast mixture and the butter mixture. Mix well. Add half the flour and beat well. Cover and let rise for 1 hour. Punch the dough down. Add the remaining flour, kneading well. Cover and let rise for 1 hour.

Roll out ½ inch thick on a lightly floured board. Spread the apples over it. Sprinkle with the cinnamon and remaining sugar. Roll up as for a jelly roll.

Butter a baking pan and dust with the bread crumbs. Place the apple roll on it, curving it if necessary to fit the pan. Let rise for 30 minutes. Preheat oven to 350°.

Bake for 50 minutes, or until browned. Sprinkle with the confectioners' sugar while hot.

Serve hot or cold.

NOODLE FRUIT PUDDING

4 egg yolks
4 tablespoons melted shortening
3 tablespoons sugar
½ teaspoon salt
1 teaspoon cinnamon
½ pound fine noodles, cooked and drained
1 apple, peeled and diced
½ cup seedless raisins
¼ cup coarsely chopped walnuts
4 egg whites

Beat the egg yolks in a bowl. Add the shortening, sugar, salt, and cinnamon. Mix well together. Add the noodles, apple, raisins, and walnuts. Mix again.

Beat the egg whites until stiff but not dry. Fold them into the previous mixture gently but thoroughly. Pour into a greased 2-quart baking dish.

Bake in a 375° oven for 40 minutes, or until set and lightly browned on top.

This is such an old-time recipe that I don't even remember where I got it. It seems I was acquainted with it all my life. I call it Television Almond Pastry because it's obvious. I mean, you could put anything on a plate and people watching television would eat it, this cake in particular. You wouldn't think that between watching and talking and the criticizing there would be time to eat, but there is. My recipe is figured for six people looking at television for an hour. Maybe it will last less or more. It's all according to the individuals. For a 2-hour show, double the recipe.

TELEVISION ALMOND PASTRY

½ pound butter
1 cup sugar
¾ cup ground almonds
1 cup sifted flour
¼ teaspoon salt
6 egg yolks

Cream the butter. Add the sugar gradually, beating until thick and light in color. Mix the almonds, flour, and salt together. Add alternately with 1 egg yolk at a time, until all have been added. Mix well. Preheat oven to 350°.

Butter a baking pan about 8 x 10 inches and dust lightly with flour. Pour the mixture into it.

Bake for 35 minutes, or until crisp and lightly browned. Cut into squares while still warm.

APPLE PASTRY

2¼ cups sugar
¾ cup water
6 apples, peeled and sliced
2 teaspoons grated lemon rind
1½ cups sifted flour
¼ teaspoon salt
¼ pound butter
1 egg
2 tablespoons heavy cream

Combine 1½ cups of the sugar and the water in a saucepan. Cook until syrupy, about 10 minutes. Add the apples and lemon rind and cook over low heat for 10 minutes longer, or until the apple slices are coated with syrup and glossy. Stir occasionally while cooking. Cool. Preheat oven to 375°.

Sift the flour, salt, and remaining sugar into a bowl. Work the butter in by hand. Beat the egg and cream together and add to the flour mixture. Mix lightly by hand until well blended. Spread on a buttered jelly-roll pan.

Bake for 25 minutes. Spread the apple mixture over the pastry. Reduce heat to 350° and bake for 20 minutes additional.

Cut into strips and serve either hot or cold.

ROSIE'S SUGAR RINGS

¾ cup sifted flour
⅛ teaspoon salt
¼ pound butter
⅔ cup sugar
4 hard-cooked egg yolks, mashed
2 teaspoons grated orange rind
3 tablespoons heavy cream
¼ cup coarsely ground walnuts

Sift the flour and salt into a bowl. Work the butter in by hand. Add ½ cup of the sugar, the egg yolks, and orange rind, kneading until well blended. Chill for 1 hour.

Preheat oven to 350°. Working quickly, break off small pieces of the dough. Roll into pencil-thin strips on a lightly floured surface. Bring the ends together to form a ring. Place on an unbuttered cooky sheet. Brush with the cream. Mix the walnuts with the remaining sugar and sprinkle on top.

Bake for 12 minutes.

SUGAR COOKIES

> 1⅛ cups sifted flour
> ⅛ teaspoon salt
> 2 teaspoons cinnamon
> ¾ cup sugar
> ¼ pound butter
> 3 eggs
> ½ cup coarsely chopped nuts
>   (walnuts, pecans, almonds)

Sift the flour, salt, 1 teaspoon of the cinnamon, and all but 2 table-spoons of the sugar into a bowl. Work the butter in by hand. Add the eggs, reserving 1 egg white. Mix until a ball of dough is formed. Chill for 1 hour. Preheat oven to 375°.

Roll out the dough about ⅛ inch thick on a lightly floured board. Cut into desired shapes. Place on a buttered cooky sheet. Brush with the reserved egg white. Mix the nuts with the remaining sugar and cinnamon and sprinkle on top.

Bake for 12 minutes, or until browned lightly and crisp.

HONEY COOKIES

> 2 eggs
> ¾ cup sugar
> ½ cup honey
> 3 cups sifted flour
> ¼ teaspoon baking soda
> 1 teaspoon cinnamon

Beat the eggs in a bowl. Add the sugar, beating until thick and light in color. Add the honey, mixing well.

Sift the flour, baking soda, and cinnamon together. Gradually add to the honey mixture, beating steadily. Preheat oven to 300°.

Grease a cooky sheet and dust lightly with flour. Drop the honey mixture onto the sheet by the tablespoonful, leaving about 1 inch between each.

Bake for 15 minutes, or until cookies are dry but not brown. Remove from the pan at once.

ALMOND CAKES

> 2 egg whites
> 1½ cups ground almonds
> ½ cup sugar
> 1 teaspoon vanilla extract

Beat the egg whites in a bowl until stiff but not dry. Add the almonds, sugar, and vanilla extract, mixing well. The dough should have a fairly thick consistency. Add additional almonds if necessary.

Roll a tablespoonful of the mixture into a ball between floured hands. Place on a lightly floured cooky sheet and flatten slightly. Set aside for 1 hour.

Preheat oven to 325°.

Bake for 20 minutes, but do not allow the cakes to brown.

PFEFFERNUESSE

PEPPERNUTS

¾ cup shortening
½ cup sugar
1 egg yolk
1 tablespoon grated orange peel
1 tablespoon grated lemon peel
½ cup chopped candied fruit
½ cup ground blanched almonds
2 tablespoons corn syrup
½ cup molasses
3 cups sifted flour
1 teaspoon baking powder
¼ teaspoon baking soda
½ teaspoon salt
⅛ teaspoon freshly ground black pepper
⅛ teaspoon nutmeg
¼ teaspoon cinnamon
¼ teaspoon ground cloves
1 teaspoon anise seeds
2 teaspoons ground cardamon seeds
⅔ cup brandy
2 tablespoons lemon juice

Cream the shortening. Add the sugar, beating until light and fluffy. Add the egg yolk, orange peel, lemon peel, candied fruit, almonds, corn syrup, and molasses. Beat well.

Sift together the flour, baking powder, baking soda, salt, pepper, nutmeg, cinnamon, cloves, anise and cardamon seeds. Add to the previous mixture alternately with the brandy and lemon juice. Beat very well. Chill for 2 hours.

Preheat oven to 350°. Shape the dough into 1-inch balls. Place on an ungreased cooky sheet.

Bake for 15 minutes, or until lightly browned.
If desired, ice with:

> 1 cup confectioners' sugar
> ¼ cup water

Mix the confectioners' sugar and water together until smooth. Spread lightly on the balls. Return to the oven for 2 minutes.

JELLY COOKIES

> ¼ pound butter
> ⅓ cup sifted sugar
> 1 egg yolk
> 1 cup sifted flour
> ⅛ teaspoon salt
> 1 teaspoon vanilla
> ½ teaspoon orange extract
> Raspberry or other fruit-flavored jelly

Cream the butter and sugar until light. Add the egg yolk, beating well. Sift flour and salt onto the mixture; mix well. Add vanilla and orange extract, mixing well. Preheat oven to 325°.

Butter a cooky sheet and dust lightly with flour. Shape the mixture into walnut-sized balls. Make a slight depression in each, and fill with ½ teaspoon of the jelly. Place on the cooky sheet, leaving ½ inch between each.

Bake 15 minutes, or until delicately browned.

CHEESE COOKIES

2 cups sifted flour
⅛ teaspoon salt
½ pound butter
½ pound cottage cheese, drained
1 egg yolk, beaten
1 egg white
⅓ cup ground blanched almonds
⅓ cup sugar

Sift the flour and salt onto a board. Work in the butter and cottage cheese. Add the egg yolk, mixing until a ball of dough is formed. Roll out and fold over in thirds. Chill for 1 hour.

Preheat oven to 375°. Roll out the dough ⅛ inch thick on a lightly floured surface. Cut into any desired shapes. Place on a cooky sheet. Brush with the egg white. Mix the almonds and sugar together and sprinkle over cookies.

Bake for 15 minutes, or until browned and crisp.

FRIED EGG KUCHEN (COOKIES)

1⅞ cups sifted flour
½ teaspoon salt
3 eggs, beaten
Fat for deep frying
½ cup confectioners' sugar

Sift the flour and salt onto a board. Make a well in the center and pour the eggs into it. Work the flour in gradually, kneading until smooth. Roll out as thin as possible. Cut into 4-x-6-inch oblongs with a pastry wheel. Cut a 2-inch gash lengthwise on one side of the oblong and pull the other end of the dough through it.

Heat the fat to 370° and drop the *kuchen* into it. Fry until lightly browned on both sides. Do not turn them more than once. Drain. Sprinkle with the confectioners' sugar while hot.

Serve warm.

MAZUREK

POLISH CHOCOLATE
SQUARES

6 squares (6 ounces) unsweetened chocolate
5 tablespoons shortening
1½ cups sugar
6 egg yolks
1½ teaspoons vanilla extract
1⅔ cups bread crumbs
6 egg whites

Melt the chocolate over hot water. Let cool. Cream the shortening. Add the sugar gradually, beating steadily. Add the egg yolks and vanilla. Mix well. Add the chocolate and mix again. Add 1½ cups of the bread crumbs and mix. Preheat oven to 350°.

Beat the egg whites until stiff but not dry. Fold them into the chocolate mixture carefully but thoroughly. Grease a jelly-roll pan, about 11 x 17 inches, and dust with the remaining bread crumbs. Pour the batter into it.

Bake for 30 minutes. Turn off the heat and allow the cake to remain in the oven for 10 minutes.

Cut into squares and serve with whipped cream if desired.

RICE CUPCAKES

1 cup sifted flour
1 tablespoon baking powder
¼ teaspoon salt
2 eggs
4 tablespoons brown sugar
1 cup cooked rice
¾ cup milk
½ teaspoon vanilla extract
2 tablespoons melted butter

Sift the flour, baking powder, and salt together.

Preheat oven to 400°. Beat the eggs well in a bowl. Add the brown sugar, beating well. Add the rice and mix. Add the milk alternately with the flour mixture, mixing well. Add the vanilla and melted butter. Beat well.

Pour into buttered muffin tins. There is enough batter for about 16 muffins.

Bake for 30 minutes, or until a cake tester comes out clean.

Yom Kippur is the Day of Atonement, a day of fasting, a day we ask forgiveness for all our sins, the day on which the good Lord writes in the book of life who shall live and who shall die. Even My Rich Cousin Simon spends the whole day in Temple and fasts from sundown to sundown. It's a day of meditation, it's a day of taking inventory of one's deeds and actions of the past year. Each year after a day in Temple, I feel like a better person.

This Spongecake is so delicious—I break my fast with it because it's feathery and light.

SPONGECAKE

6 egg yolks
1½ cups sifted sugar
2 tablespoons ice water
2 teaspoons lemon juice
1 teaspoon grated lemon rind
1 teaspoon vanilla extract
¼ teaspoon salt
6 egg whites
1½ cups sifted flour

Beat the egg yolks in a bowl. Gradually add the sugar, beating until thick and light in color. Add the ice water, lemon juice, lemon rind, and vanilla. Mix well. Preheat oven to 325°.

Sprinkle the salt on the egg whites. Beat until stiff but not dry. Place on top of the egg yolk mixture. Sift the flour on top. Fold in carefully but thoroughly.

Grease an angel-cake pan and dust lightly with flour. Pour the batter into it.

Bake for 50 minutes, or until a cake tester comes out clean. Invert the pan and let cool.

SPONGECAKE LAYERS

6 egg yolks
⅓ cup sifted sugar
⅓ cup sifted flour
½ teaspoon baking powder
⅛ teaspoon salt
1 teaspoon vanilla extract
6 egg whites

Grease 2 9-inch layer-cake pans and dust with flour.

Beat the egg yolks in a bowl. Add the sugar, beating until thick and light in color. Sift the flour, baking powder, and salt together and add. Add vanilla and mix well. Preheat oven to 350°.

Beat the egg whites until stiff but not dry. Fold into the egg yolk mixture carefully. Pour into the layer-cake pans.

Bake for 20 minutes, or until a cake tester comes out clean.

The cakes may be iced, used for shortcakes, or served plain.

NUT SPONGECAKE

6 egg yolks
1¾ cups sifted sugar
½ teaspoon salt
1½ cups matzo meal
½ cup sifted potato starch
1 cup orange juice, strained
1 cup ground walnuts
2 tablespoons grated orange rind
6 egg whites

Beat the egg yolks. Add the sugar and salt, beating until thick and light in color. Mix the matzo meal and potato starch together and add alternately with the orange juice. Mix well. Add the nuts and orange rind and mix well again. Preheat oven to 325°.

Beat the egg whites until stiff but not dry. Fold into the nut mixture carefully but thoroughly. Pour into an ungreased angel-cake pan.

Bake for 1 hour, or until a cake tester comes out clean.

This cake may be served during Passover.

LEMON SPONGECAKE

1 cup sugar
⅓ cup water
5 egg whites
5 egg yolks
3 tablespoons lemon juice
2 teaspoons grated lemon rind
½ teaspoon salt
⅞ cup sifted flour

Boil the sugar and water together until a thread forms when a fork is lifted from the pan, about 10 minutes.

Beat the egg whites until stiff but not dry. Pour the hot sugar syrup into them slowly, mixing steadily.

Beat the egg yolks until thick. Add the lemon juice, lemon rind, and salt. Mix. Preheat oven to 325°.

Combine both mixtures carefully. Fold in the flour carefully but thoroughly. Pour into an angel-cake pan that has been greased and dusted with flour.

Bake for 40 minutes, or until a cake tester comes out clean. Invert pan until cool.

KOMISHBROT

TOASTED ALMOND CAKE SLICES

4 eggs
1 cup sugar
2 tablespoons salad oil
½ teaspoon almond extract
½ teaspoon vanilla extract
1 cup sifted flour
1 teaspoon baking powder
¼ teaspoon salt
1 cup blanched almonds
3 teaspoons cinnamon

229

Beat the eggs in a bowl. Add the sugar, beating until thick and light in color. Add the oil, almond and vanilla extracts. Mix well. Sift the flour, baking powder, and salt together and add, mixing well. Add the almonds. Preheat oven to 350°.

Pour a quarter of the mixture into a 12-inch oiled loaf pan. Sprinkle with 1 teaspoon of the cinnamon. Repeat the process twice more.

Bake for 40 minutes, or until a cake tester comes out clean. Remove from the pan. Cool for 15 minutes. Cut into ½-inch slices. Place on a cooky sheet and put under the broiler until delicately browned on both sides. Let cool.

I don't know how many people make their own strudel any more, but it is one of the experiences of life that I wouldn't miss. Why? Because. To make strudel you need a family. You need them to help stretch the dough so thin that you can read through it, and you need them to help fold the dough and roll it, and then you need them to help you eat it. Of course this is not the only reason for a family, and for my family I would even give up strudel but they wouldn't let me. For strudel, they say, you need a mother. Nu? That's a family for you.

STRUDEL

> 1½ cups sifted flour
> ¼ teaspoon salt
> 1 egg white
> 3 tablespoons salad oil
> ⅓ cup lukewarm water
> 2 teaspoons vinegar
> ¼ cup melted shortening

Sift the flour and salt onto a board. Make a well in the center. Place the egg white, 1 tablespoon salad oil, the water, and vinegar in it. Work in the flour, kneading until a dough is formed. Pick up the dough and slap it down hard several times. Knead it until it is elastic. Brush with remaining oil. Cover with a warm bowl for 30 minutes.

Cover a large surface, such as a table, with a tablecloth and dust with flour. Roll out the dough until about ¼ inch thick. Brush with a little melted shortening. Stretch the dough as thin as possible, using lightly floured hands. Place the hands under the dough and pull it to you gently and carefully, using only the back of your hands. Go around the table, pulling the dough toward you, so that the dough is stretched as thin as possible. A few small holes in the dough are unimportant. The dough should be transparent; cut off any thick edges. Brush with the remaining melted shortening. Preheat oven to 425°.

Spread any desired filling over the dough and roll up carefully (by gently lifting one side of the tablecloth) as for a jelly roll. Place on a greased baking pan, cutting the *strudel* to fit, if necessary.

Bake for 40 minutes, or until *strudel* is crisp and brown. Serve hot or cold.

CHEESE FILLING
FOR STRUDEL

> ½ pound cream cheese
> ½ pound cottage cheese, drained
> ½ cup sugar
> 2 tablespoons sour cream
> 1 teaspoon vanilla extract
> ¼ cup seedless raisins (optional)
> 3 tablespoons melted butter

Beat the cream cheese and cottage cheese together until smooth. Add the sugar, sour cream, and vanilla. Add the raisins. Mix. Sprinkle the butter on the dough and spread the cheese mixture over it.

Proceed as directed for *strudel*.

DRIED FRUIT FILLING
FOR STRUDEL

1 pound prunes, pitted and
   chopped
1 cup chopped dates
1 cup chopped dried apricots or
   pears
1 cup chopped apple
3 tablespoons lemon juice
2 teaspoons grated lemon rind
¼ cup honey
⅓ cup sugar

Combine the prunes, dates, apricots, apple, lemon juice, lemon rind, honey, and sugar. Mix until well blended.
   Proceed as directed for *strudel*.

APPLE FILLING
FOR STRUDEL

1 cup ground walnuts
¼ cup bread crumbs
8 apples, peeled and sliced
¾ cup sugar
¼ cup seedless raisins
¼ cup chopped candied fruit
   (optional)

Mix the walnuts and bread crumbs together. Spread over the dough. Mix the apples, sugar, raisins, and candied fruit. Spread over the nuts.
   Proceed as directed for *strudel*.

CHERRY FILLING
FOR STRUDEL

1½ cups sour red cherries, fresh,
   frozen, or canned
1 cup sugar
¾ cup bread crumbs
3 tablespoons melted shortening

Pit the cherries and drain them. Add the sugar, mixing well. Sprinkle
the bread crumbs and shortening over the dough. Spread with the
cherries, but not too close to the edges.

Proceed as directed for *strudel*.

MOHN FILLING
FOR STRUDEL

½ cup milk
½ cup honey
2 tablespoons sugar
1 pound ground poppy seeds
¼ cup seedless raisins
2 teaspoons grated lemon rind
4 tablespoons melted butter

Mix the milk, honey, sugar, and poppy seeds in a saucepan. Cook
over low heat until thickened, about 5 minutes. Add the raisins and
lemon rind. Mix. Cool.

Spread the filling on the dough, and sprinkle with the melted butter. Proceed as directed for *strudel*.

*If there's one thing that smells good when it's baking
it's a nut cake. You can use any nuts howsoever. But filberts
(hazelnuts, they sometimes call them) are the best. Without*

233

a fraction of a doubt this Nut Cake is three ways better than anything. In the first place, when it cooks, the aroma is more than delicious. In the second place, when you eat it, it's a treat of the first order, and in the third place the compliments are worth more than anything put together. So from this cake you can choose any of these three things you desire and then you can eat the cake too, and that's a very high accomplishment. And, oh yes, to get a good flavor you should also buy nuts in the shell and crack yourself.

NUT CAKE

8 egg yolks
1¼ cups sifted sugar
2 cups ground nuts (hazelnuts, Brazil nuts, or almonds)
½ teaspoon instant-coffee powder
1 tablespoon bread crumbs or matzo meal
2 tablespoons brandy
8 egg whites

Beat the egg yolks very well. Add the sugar, beating until thick and light in color. Add the ground nuts, coffee powder, bread crumbs, and brandy. Mix well. Preheat oven to 350°.

Beat the egg whites until stiff but not dry. Fold into the nut mixture carefully but thoroughly.

Grease a 9-inch spring-form and dust lightly with bread crumbs. Pour the batter into it.

Bake for 40 minutes, or until a cake tester comes out clean. Cool and then carefully remove the sides of the spring-form.

If desired, the cake may be split in half and filled and covered with whipped cream.

May also be used for Passover.

APPLE AUFLAUF (SOUFFLE CAKE)

3 tablespoons butter
⅓ cup brown sugar
4 apples, peeled and sliced
3 egg yolks
⅔ cup sugar
1 tablespoon cold water
⅔ cup sifted flour
¾ teaspoon baking powder
¼ cup ground blanched almonds
1 teaspoon vanilla extract
3 egg whites

Spread the butter on the bottom and sides of a 2-quart casserole. Spread half of the brown sugar over it. Arrange the apples in layers and sprinkle with the remaining brown sugar. Bake in a 350° oven for 15 minutes. Remove from the oven and let cool for 30 minutes. Preheat oven to 350° again.

Beat the egg yolks in a bowl. Add the sugar and water, beating until light in color. Sift the flour and baking powder together and add, mixing well. Add the almonds and vanilla and mix again.

Beat the egg whites until stiff but not dry. Fold them into the previous mixture carefully. Pour over the apples.

Bake for 30 minutes, or until a cake tester comes out clean. Serve hot.

This is a superstitious recipe. Some mornings I get up singing my favorite waltz by Strauss, and when I hear myself singing I know there's going to be company, so I make this cake. A long time ago it was called a Sand Torte by a dear Viennese friend from Vienna. I call it Strauss Waltz Butter Cake because of the singing. Sometimes company comes, sometimes not, but by the end of the evening do you think there's a drop left? Not one snitch even.

STRAUSS WALTZ BUTTER CAKE

½ pound butter
1¼ cups sifted sugar
½ cup sifted potato starch
½ cup sifted cornstarch
1 cup sifted flour
1 tablespoon baking powder
4 eggs
2 teaspoons vanilla extract

Preheat oven to 375°.

Cream the butter; add the sugar, beating until light and smooth. Sift the potato starch, cornstarch, flour, and baking powder together. Add ½ cup at a time, alternating with one egg at a time, beating well after each addition. Add the vanilla, beating well.

Pour into a buttered angel-cake pan, spreading the batter very evenly.

Bake 40 minutes, or until a cake tester comes out clean.

Remove from pan, cool, and sprinkle with confectioners' sugar if desired.

PLUM CAKE

2 cups sifted flour
¼ teaspoon salt
½ teaspoon baking powder
¾ cup sugar
¼ pound butter
2 egg yolks, beaten
2 tablespoons heavy cream
18 small blue plums, pitted and
    halved
2 teaspoons cinnamon
    (optional)

Sift the flour, salt, baking powder, and ½ cup of the sugar into a bowl. Work the butter in by hand. Mix the egg yolks and cream together and add, mixing until a ball of dough is formed. Chill for 1 hour.

Roll out the dough to fit a 10-x-16-inch baking pan. Form a ridge around the edges. Preheat oven to 375°. Arrange the plums in even rows on the dough. Mix the remaining sugar and cinnamon together and sprinkle over the plums.

Bake in a 375° oven for 15 minutes. Reduce heat to 350° and bake for 30 minutes longer.

Serve hot or cold.

SCHAUM TORTE

STRAWBERRY TART

6 egg whites
2 cups sugar
¼ teaspoon almond extract
1 teaspoon vanilla extract
1 tablespoon vinegar
2 cups strawberries
2 cups whipped cream

Beat the egg whites until stiff but not dry. Very gradually add ½ cup of the sugar, beating constantly. Add the almond and vanilla extracts and vinegar. Fold in 1 cup of the sugar thoroughly. Preheat oven to 275°.

Grease a 9-inch spring-form pan and dust lightly with flour. Pour the mixture into it.

Bake for 1¼ hours, or until firm and delicately browned. Cool. Remove from the spring-form carefully.

Sprinkle the remaining sugar on the berries. Cover the torte with whipped cream and arrange the berries on top.

The torte makes a very good Passover dessert. Sprinkle spring-form pan with potato starch instead of flour, if used for that purpose.

JAM TART

1 cup sifted flour
½ teaspoon salt
¼ pound butter
½ cup sour cream
1½ cups jam or preserves
1 egg yolk
½ teaspoon almond extract
½ cup heavy cream
1½ cups ground walnuts

Sift the flour and salt into a bowl. Work the butter in by hand. Add 3 tablespoons of the sour cream, mixing until a ball of dough is formed. Chill for 2 hours, or overnight if possible.

Roll out the dough on a lightly floured surface. Fit the dough into a 9-inch pie plate. Flute the edges with a fork. Spread the jam on the bottom. Preheat oven to 400°.

Beat the egg yolk, almond extract, heavy cream, and remaining sour cream together. Add the walnuts and mix. Smooth the mixture over the jam.

Bake for 25 minutes, or until browned.

RHUBARB COMPOTE

12 stalks rhubarb
⅔ cup sugar

Wash the rhubarb; scrape lightly and discard leaves. (It is not necessary to peel rhubarb, merely remove the long fibers, if any.) Cut into ½-inch pieces.

Combine in a skillet or saucepan with the sugar; do not add any water. Cook over low heat for 10 minutes, or until the rhubarb is soft. Taste for sweetening, adding a little more sugar if necessary.

Serve cold.

APPLE COMPOTE

1¼ cups sugar
2 cups water
2 teaspoons cinnamon
8 apples, peeled and quartered

Combine the sugar, water, and cinnamon in a saucepan. Boil for 5 minutes. Add the apples and cook over low heat for 10 minutes, or until apples are transparent. Turn the apples frequently.

Chill. Serve as an accompaniment to meat dishes or as a dessert.

How can I give a definition of Rosh Hashonah? It would not suffice it to say that this is the holiday which marks the beginning of the New Year, and it also would not be enough to say that Rosh Hashonah is the beginning of ten days of prayer. All these things it is, but it's more. It's the time when we pray the good Lord to be merciful and give us a favorable judgment on the tenth day of meditation, which is the Day of Atonement.

In the evening, when families visit after the holiday is over, when everyone is looking forward to a sweet year, I like to serve honey cake—it's a proper beginning for the New Year.

LEKACH

HONEY CAKE

2 eggs
½ cup sugar
¼ cup freshly brewed coffee
½ cup honey
1 tablespoon salad oil
1¾ cups sifted flour
⅛ teaspoon salt
¾ teaspoon baking powder
½ teaspoon baking soda
1 cup coarsely chopped nuts
   (filberts, almonds, or walnuts)
2 tablespoons brandy (optional)

Beat the eggs in a bowl. Add the sugar and beat until light and fluffy. Mix the coffee, honey, and salad oil together and combine with the eggs. Sift the flour, salt, baking powder, and baking soda together. Add the nuts and stir. Gradually add to the egg mixture, stirring constantly. Add the brandy and stir. Preheat oven to 325°.

Oil a loaf pan and line it carefully with wax paper or aluminum foil. Pour the batter into it. Bake for 45 minutes, or until a cake tester comes out clean. Remove cake from the oven and allow to cool thoroughly in the pan. Remove carefully.

BAKED WINE DESSERT

6 eggs
3 tablespoons cold water
1 teaspoon salt
4 tablespoons shortening
¾ cup sugar
3 tablespoons cinnamon
2½ cups sweet red wine

Beat the eggs, water, and salt together.

Melt 1 tablespoon of the shortening in a 9-inch skillet. Pour ¼ cup of the egg mixture into it, turning the pan quickly to coat the bottom. Cook over low heat until lightly browned on both sides. Stack the omelets while preparing the balance. Add additional shortening as necessary. Sprinkle each omelet with sugar and cinnamon and roll up. Preheat oven to 350°.

Arrange the omelets in a greased casserole or baking dish. Pour the wine over them.

Bake for 50 minutes, or until the wine is almost absorbed.

Serve hot with additional sugar and cinnamon as desired.

FRUIT AND NUT COMPOTE

1 pound unsweetened prunes, presoaked
1 pound assorted dried fruits (pears, apricots, peaches, etc.), presoaked
1½ cups water
¾ cup sugar
1 lemon, sliced thin
¼ pound blanched almonds

Combine the prunes, assorted dried fruits, water, sugar, and lemon slices in a saucepan. Bring to a boil. Cover and cook over low heat for 15 minutes. Add the almonds. Cook for 10 minutes. Add a little more sugar if necessary.

Chill and serve.

FRUIT KISSEL

JELLED FRUIT DESSERT

2 cups raspberries, fresh or frozen
2 cups currants, cleaned
2 cups water
4 tablespoons cornstarch
¾ cup sugar

Combine the raspberries, currants, and 1¾ cups of the water in a saucepan. Boil for 10 minutes. Force through a sieve and return to saucepan.

Mix the cornstarch and remaining water to a smooth paste and add, together with the sugar. Cook, stirring constantly, until the boiling point. Cook over low heat until thick, about 5 minutes. Pour into a glass bowl or into individual dessert dishes. Chill.

Serve cold, with whipped cream if desired.

NOTE: *Kissel* is also prepared with combinations of other fresh fruits.

CRANBERRY KISSEL

JELLED CRANBERRY DESSERT

1 pound cranberries
4 cups water
2 cups sugar
2 tablespoons cornstarch

Combine the cranberries, 3½ cups of the water, and the sugar in a saucepan. Bring to a boil and cook over medium heat for 10 minutes, or until the cranberries split open. Force them through a sieve and return to the saucepan.

242

Mix the cornstarch and remaining water together until smooth. Add to the cranberries, mixing constantly until the boiling point. Cook over low heat for 5 minutes. Chill.

Serve with sweet cream or with whipped cream if desired.

FRUIT TZIMMES

> 1 pound prunes, presoaked and pitted
> ½ pound dried apricots, presoaked
> ½ pound dried pears or apples, presoaked
> 2 cups water
> 2 tablespoons honey
> 3 tablespoons brown sugar
> ¼ teaspoon salt
> ½ teaspoon cinnamon
> 3 tablespoons rice

Combine the prunes, apricots, pears, water, honey, brown sugar, salt, and cinnamon in a saucepan. Bring to a boil. Add the rice. Cook over low heat for 25 minutes, or until the liquid is absorbed. Stir occasionally.

Serve as a compote or as a dessert.

PRUNE TZIMMES

1 pound prunes, presoaked and
  pitted
⅔ cup brown sugar
3 cups water
¾ cup *farfel*, homemade (see
  recipe), or in packaged form
⅓ cup shortening
1 teaspoon salt
2 tablespoons lemon juice
2 teaspoons grated lemon rind

Combine the prunes, brown sugar, and water in a saucepan. Bring
to a boil. Add the *farfel*, shortening, salt, lemon juice, and lemon
rind. Cover and cook over medium heat for 30 minutes. Mix frequently, adding a little boiling water if necessary.

Serve as a compote or as an accompaniment to meat or poultry
dishes.

DATE TORTE

8 egg yolks
1½ cups sugar
3 tablespoons flour
2 cups chopped dates
2 cups chopped walnuts
8 egg whites

Beat the egg yolks in a bowl. Add the sugar, beating until thick and
light in color. Sprinkle the flour on the dates, tossing lightly. Add the
dates to the egg yolks, together with the nuts. Mix well. Preheat
oven to 325°.

Beat the egg whites until stiff but not dry. Fold them into the date
mixture.

Grease a 9-inch spring-form pan and dust lightly with flour. Pour the mixture into it.

Bake for 40 minutes. Cool.

Decorate with whipped cream if desired.

BERRY BLINTZES

BERRY-FILLED PANCAKES

2 eggs
1½ cups sour cream
½ cup milk
¼ teaspoon salt
2 cups sifted flour
4 tablespoons butter
⅓ cup sugar
2 cups sliced strawberries (or blueberries)

Beat the eggs, sour cream, milk, and salt together. Add the flour, beating until smooth.

Melt a little butter in a 7-inch skillet. Pour a tablespoon of the batter into it, turning the pan quickly to coat the bottom. Fry until delicately browned on both sides. Stack the *blintzes* while preparing the balance. Use additional butter as required. Preheat oven to 475°.

Sprinkle the sugar on the berries, mixing well. Place a heaping tablespoon of the berries on each pancake and roll up, turning in the sides. Place on a buttered baking sheet.

Bake for 5 minutes. Serve hot.

*If you like surprises, this recipe will fulfill your craving.
Not only will you be surprised by the way it tastes and looks,
but your whole family will be able to join you. And when you*

tell them it's made with carrots they will be unbelievable. Take my word.

CARROT CAKE

> 5 carrots, peeled
> 1 cup water
> 9 egg yolks
> 2 cups sifted sugar
> 1 tablespoon grated orange rind
> 1 tablespoon brandy
> 3 cups ground almonds
> 9 egg whites

Combine the carrots and water in a saucepan. Cook over low heat for 15 minutes, or until very tender. Drain and mash. Let cool.

Beat the egg yolks in a bowl. Add the sugar, beating until thick and light in color. Add the carrots, orange rind, brandy, and almonds. Mix lightly. Preheat oven to 325°.

Beat the egg whites until stiff but not dry. Fold into the nut mixture carefully but thoroughly. Pour into a 9-inch greased spring-form pan.

Bake for 50 minutes, or until a cake tester comes out clean. Cool. Serve with whipped cream if desired.

PRUNE PUDDING

1 pound prunes, pitted,
  presoaked
1¼ cups water
¾ cup sugar
¼ cup cornstarch
¼ cup coarsely chopped almonds
2 tablespoons lemon juice

Combine the prunes, 1 cup of the water, and the sugar in a saucepan. Cook over low heat for 15 minutes. Mix the cornstarch and remaining water until smooth and add to the prunes, stirring constantly until the boiling point. Cook over low heat for 10 minutes additional, stirring frequently. Add the almonds and lemon juice. Mix well. Pour into a glass bowl or individual molds.

Chill. Serve with whipped cream if desired.

COTTAGE CHEESE CAKE

18 zwiebach
1½ cups sugar
¼ pound butter, melted
2 cups cottage cheese
¼ cup sifted flour
4 eggs
¼ teaspoon salt
1 cup heavy cream
2 tablespoons lemon juice
1 teaspoon grated lemon rind
1 teaspoon vanilla extract

Mix the zwiebach and ½ cup of the sugar together. Add the butter and mix. Spread on the bottom of a 9-inch spring-form pan, packing down well.

Mix the cottage cheese and flour together and force through a sieve. (If an electric mixer is used for the following steps, it need not be forced through a sieve.) Preheat oven to 250°.

Beat the eggs and salt together. Add the remaining sugar, beating until thick and light in color. Add the cheese mixture, heavy cream, lemon juice, lemon rind, and vanilla. Beat well. Pour into the spring form.

Bake for 1 hour. Turn off the heat, but allow the cake to remain in the oven with the door closed for 1 hour longer. Cool and remove sides of spring-form pan. Chill.

CHEESE PUDDING

¼ pound cream cheese
¾ pound cottage cheese, drained
3 egg yolks
⅛ teaspoon salt
1 cup sugar
⅓ cup melted butter
1 teaspoon vanilla extract
3 tablespoons flour
3 hard-cooked egg yolks, finely
chopped
½ cup seedless raisins
3 egg whites

Force the cream cheese and cottage cheese through a sieve. Beat the egg yolks in a bowl. Add the salt and sugar, beating until thick and light in color. Add the butter, vanilla, flour, chopped egg yolks, raisins, and the cheese. Mix together very well. Preheat oven to 325°.

Beat the egg whites until stiff but not dry. Fold them into the cheese mixture carefully but thoroughly. Pour into a buttered 1½-quart baking dish.

Bake for 35 minutes, or until firm and lightly browned. Serve hot or cold.

RUGLACH

CREAM CHEESE PASTRIES

1 cup sifted flour
¼ teaspoon salt
¼ pound sweet butter
¼ pound cream cheese
1 egg white, stiffly beaten
¾ cup ground walnuts
¼ cup sugar
1 tablespoon cinnamon

Sift the flour and salt into a bowl. Work the butter and cream cheese in by hand. Roll out onto a lightly floured board. Fold into thirds and chill overnight, or at least 2 hours.

Preheat oven to 375°. Roll out the dough ⅛ inch thick. Cut into 4-inch squares. Mix the egg white, walnuts, sugar, and cinnamon together. Spread 1 tablespoon of the mixture on one corner of each square, and roll up diagonally from that corner. Turn the ends slightly toward each other to form a crescent. Place on a baking sheet.

Bake for 20 minutes, or until delicately browned. If desired, *ruglach* may be made with a poppy seed filling, prepared as follows:

¼ cup poppy seeds
2 tablespoons chopped apple
2 tablespoons ground nuts
3 tablespoons sugar

Mix the poppy seeds, apple, nuts, and sugar together and proceed as directed above.

RICE PUDDING

4 eggs
¼ cup sugar
½ cup sour cream
3 cups cooked rice
¼ cup ground blanched almonds
1 teaspoon grated lemon rind

Beat the eggs; add the sugar, beating until thick and light. Add the sour cream, rice, almonds, and lemon rind. Mix well. Preheat the oven to 350°.

Pour the pudding into a buttered baking dish.

Bake 30 minutes, or until lightly browned and set.

Serve warm or cold.

SOUR CREAM CAKE

4 eggs
1½ cups sugar
1 cup sour cream
1 teaspoon vanilla extract
1¾ cups sifted flour
2 tablespoons potato starch
1 teaspoon baking powder
1 teaspoon baking soda
½ cup ground nuts (almonds, walnuts, hazelnuts)
2 teaspoons cinnamon

Beat the eggs in a bowl. Add the sugar, beating until thick and light in color. Add the sour cream and vanilla. Sift the flour, potato starch, baking powder, and baking soda together and add. Beat until smooth. Preheat oven to 375°.

Pour half the batter into a 10-inch buttered loaf pan. Sprinkle the nuts and cinnamon on it and cover with the remaining batter.

Bake for 45 minutes, or until a cake tester comes out clean.

CHEESE KUCHEN

CHEESE PUDDING CAKE

1 cup sifted flour
¼ teaspoon salt
¼ pound butter
3 tablespoons sour cream
½ pound cottage cheese
¼ pound cream cheese
1 tablespoon cornstarch
2 tablespoons heavy cream
3 egg yolks
¾ cup sugar
1 teaspoon vanilla extract
3 tablespoons seedless raisins
3 egg whites
½ cup sliced blanched almonds

Sift the flour and salt into a bowl. Work the butter in by hand. Add the sour cream, mixing until a ball of dough is formed. Chill overnight, or at least 2 hours.

Roll out the dough as thin as possible, to fit a 9-inch pie plate. Flute the edges with a fork.

Force the cottage and cream cheese through a sieve, or beat in an electric mixer until smooth. Add the cornstarch, cream, egg yolks, and sugar. Beat well. Add the vanilla and raisins and mix well. Preheat oven to 350°.

Beat the egg whites until stiff but not dry. Fold them into the cheese mixture carefully. Pour into the prepared pie plate. Sprinkle with the almonds.

Bake for 50 minutes. Chill and serve.

This is indeed a sight for the ears. When it's blowing cold outside and the snow is dropping by the window, there isn't a nicer sound than the rice frittering in a pan of bubbling fat. It's beautiful to behold.

RICE FRITTERS

1 cup sifted flour
1 tablespoon baking powder
½ teaspoon mace
3 eggs
½ cup sugar
¼ teaspoon salt
1 cup cooked rice
Fat for deep frying
½ cup confectioners' sugar

Sift the flour, baking powder, and mace together.

Beat the eggs in a bowl. Add the sugar and salt, beating until thick and light in color. Add the rice and the flour mixture. Beat well.

Heat the fat to 375°. Drop the fritter batter by the teaspoonful into it. Fry until browned, about 3 minutes. Drain well.

Sprinkle with confectioners' sugar and serve hot.

APPLE FRITTERS

1 cup sifted flour
½ teaspoon salt
1 teaspoon baking powder
2 tablespoons sugar
1 egg
¾ cup milk
1 tablespoon brandy
2 tablespoons melted butter
4 apples, cored, peeled, and sliced
  ½ inch thick
6 tablespoons butter
½ cup confectioners' sugar

Sift the flour, salt, baking powder, and sugar into a bowl. Beat the egg, milk, and brandy together and add, beating until smooth. Add the melted butter and mix. Dip the apple slices into it, coating them well.

Melt half the butter in a skillet. Fry the fritters in it over low heat until browned on both sides. Add more butter as required. Sprinkle with the confectioners' sugar.

Serve hot.

APPLE PANCAKES

3 tablespoons lemon juice
3 apples, peeled and sliced thin
1 cup sifted flour
½ teaspoon salt
1 tablespoon sugar
4 eggs
1¼ cups milk
4 tablespoons butter

Sprinkle the lemon juice on the apples.

Sift the flour, salt, and sugar into a bowl. Beat the eggs and add the milk, mixing well. Add the egg mixture to the flour mixture, beating until smooth. Fold in the apples.

Melt 1 tablespoon of the butter in a 7-inch skillet. Pour about ½ cup of the batter into it. Fry until set and lightly browned on both sides. Repeat until all the batter is used. Add additional butter as required. If desired, larger pans may be used and larger pancakes made.

Serve with sugar and cinnamon.

MRS. L.'S MOTHER-IN-LAW'S SPICE CAKE

¼ pound butter
2 cups dark brown sugar
3 eggs
2 cups sifted flour
¼ teaspoon salt
1 teaspoon baking soda
2 teaspoons cinnamon
2 teaspoons ground allspice
½ teaspoon ground cloves
1 cup sour cream

Cream the butter; add the brown sugar, beating until light and fluffy. Add one egg at a time, beating well after each addition. Preheat oven to 350°.

Sift together the flour, salt, baking soda, cinnamon, allspice, and cloves. Add to the egg mixture alternately with the sour cream. Beat well.

Pour into two buttered 9-inch layer-cake pans.

Bake 30 minutes, or until a cake tester comes out clean.

Cool. Spread whipped cream between layers and over top of the cake, or ice with the following butter cream:

2 cups sifted confectioners' sugar
¼ cup melted butter
¾ cup heavy cream

Mix the sugar and butter together. Add enough cream to make a spreadable mixture. Ice the cake.

Holidays

No matter what Mr. Webster says about the meaning of the word "holiday," his dictionary can't ever tell you what it really is. Words are not enough to describe a feeling, and for my family to come together to celebrate a holiday, any holiday, is an occasion, a bigger occasion than Mr. Webster even dreamed about in his dictionary.

Beginning with New Year's, the calendar goes around from Lincoln's Birthday to Valentine's Day to Washington's Birthday to St. Patrick's Day. Then follow Purim and Lent, close together, and in my neighborhood you'd be surprised how the recipes change from hand to hand and back and forth. For Easter and Passover, which follow next, I always plan for a big table because from out of town and the four corners I never know who is going to drop in from where. The unexpected is always welcome and a full house is always a pleasure.

Decoration Day starts our neighborhood on the picnic season and the Fourth of July is next, when the Parents and Teachers and all the children have their annual. And then, very sad to say, the summer closes with Labor Day. Then we have Rosh Hashonah and Yom Kippur, and before you can turn over Thanksgiving has come around the corner.

After that come Chanukah and Christmas and the presents from one to another and good will and peace and the *happiness to share with the family and all our friends. In our own way my neighbors and all our families live in peace and deep friendship that extends beyond ourselves and goes forth to the world.*

And then comes the next holiday on the calendar pad and it all starts all over again. You would think there were enough holidays to celebrate for one year, but for me, I could double the recipe and then maybe there would be enough. Maybe, but not positively.

PRUNE HAMMENTASHEN

PRUNE CAKES

¾ cup sugar
2 cups sifted flour
2 teaspoons baking powder
¼ teaspoon salt
½ cup shortening
1 egg, beaten
2 tablespoons orange juice

Sift the sugar, flour, baking powder, and salt into a bowl. Work the shortening in by hand. Add the egg and orange juice, mixing until a dough is formed. Chill overnight if possible, or at least 2 hours. Now prepare the filling:

1 pound unsweetened prunes,
  presoaked, pitted, and chopped
3 tablespoons water
1 tablespoon lemon juice
½ cup honey
2 teaspoons grated lemon rind
¼ cup ground almonds or
  hazelnuts (filberts)

Combine the prunes and water in a saucepan. Cook over low heat for 10 minutes. Add the lemon juice and honey. Cook until thickened, about 5 minutes, stirring frequently. Add the lemon rind and nuts. Mix together. Remove from heat and let cool.

Roll out the dough about ⅛ inch thick on a lightly floured board. Cut into 3-inch circles. Place 1 heaping teaspoonful of the prune mixture on each. Pinch 3 edges of the dough together, but leave a small opening in the center; the resulting pastry will be in the shape of a triangle with a little of the filling showing. Place on a greased cooky sheet. Cover with a cloth and set aside for ½ hour.

Preheat oven to 400°.

Bake for 20 minutes, or until delicately browned on top.

This is My Uncle David's recipe, exclusive. Every time he makes it he tells us the story of Haman and Queen Esther. To hear him, you would think he was there, and no matter how many times Jake has heard the story and myself and the children, we can hear it again. Purim is called the Feast of Esther, who was King Ahasuerus' Queen. She saved the Jewish people from destruction by Haman, their enemy. Children love this holiday, because it is a little like Halloween. They dress up in costumes and act out the story. Uncle David acts it out too, that's why when he makes Hammentaschen, nobody would miss it for the world.

UNCLE DAVID'S
POPPY-SEED HAMMENTASHEN

> 1 cake or package yeast
> 1¼ cups scalded milk, cooled to
>   lukewarm
> ½ cup sugar
> ½ cup shortening, melted
> ½ teaspoon salt
> 2 eggs, beaten
> 3¾ cups sifted flour

Combine the yeast, ¼ cup of the milk, and 3 tablespoons of the sugar in a cup. Allow to soften for 5 minutes.

Combine the remaining milk and sugar, shortening, salt, eggs, and the yeast mixture in a bowl. Add the flour gradually, mixing together lightly until a dough is formed. Knead until very smooth. Place in a greased bowl, cover with a cloth, and set aside in a warm place for 2 hours, or until double in bulk. Now prepare the filling:

> 2 cups poppy seeds, ground (see
>   note below)
> ¾ cup milk
> ½ cup honey
> ¼ cup brown sugar
> ⅛ teaspoon salt
> 1 egg, beaten
> 1 egg yolk

Combine the poppy seeds, milk, honey, brown sugar, and salt in a saucepan. Cook over low heat until thick, about 5 minutes, stirring almost constantly. Let cool for 15 minutes. Add the egg and mix well.

Punch down the dough and knead for 1 minute. Roll out about ⅛-inch thick on a lightly floured surface. Cut into 3-inch circles. Place 1 heaping teaspoonful of the poppy-seed mixture on each. Pinch 3 edges of the dough together, but leave a small opening in the center; the resulting pastry will be in the shape of a triangle, with a little of the filling showing. Place on a greased cooky sheet. Cover with a cloth and set aside for 1 hour.

Preheat oven to 350°. Brush the tops of the pastry with the egg yolk.

Bake for 20 minutes, or until delicately browned on top.

> NOTE: If possible, have the poppy seeds ground at the store where they are purchased. They may be readily ground at home by pouring boiling water over them and letting them stand for 10 minutes. Drain very well and put them through a food chopper or mill.

This candy we have but once a year for Purim, and you would think that I had more than two children in the house when it came time to make the candy. Rosie and Sammy I could understand when they could hardly wait for me to pour the candy, but such big babies as Jake and David you never saw. They would all stand around the table waiting for the candy to get hard so they could have a little taste, and it never got hard enough for them. I don't know what gets into them on the holidays, but would I be disappointed if they didn't get excited? I should so say so.

MOHN CANDY

POPPY-SEED CANDY

½ cup sugar
2 cups honey
2 pounds poppy seeds
2 cups hazel nuts (filberts) or almonds, halved

Combine the sugar, honey, and poppy seeds in a saucepan. Cook over low heat until thick, about 30 minutes. Stir frequently. Add the nuts and mix well.

Wet a wooden board and pour the mixture onto it. Pat down until about ½ inch thick. Cool. Cut with a wet knife into diamond-shaped pieces about 2 inches long. When thoroughly cool, lift the pieces with a knife and place on a lightly floured platter.

The candy will keep indefinitely.

If you have a daughter like My Rosie and she's My Rosie's age, then this is a good recipe for you. I find that sometimes my daughter is walking around the house without her head. I don't have to ask the trouble, I know already there's a boy someplace. I also know it's a good time to make teiglach *even if it's not* Purim, *because after the dough is made and cooked I can sit Rosie down and have her roll the dough in honey and nuts and she doesn't even know what she's doing. Sammy says it's therapy. I say it's smart. Jake and David say it's good, and Rosie wants to know when did she make* teiglach?

ROSIE'S TEIGLACH

HONEY-NUT PASTRY

2 cups sifted flour
½ teaspoon salt
½ teaspoon baking powder
2 eggs, beaten
3 tablespoons salad oil
1 cup honey
½ cup brown sugar
½ teaspoon powdered ginger
1 cup hazelnuts (filberts)

Sift the flour, salt, and baking powder onto a board. Make a well in the center. Pour the eggs and oil into it. Work in the flour gradually until a soft dough is formed. Knead until smooth. Roll between lightly floured hands into strips the thickness of a cigarette. Cut into ½-inch lengths. Place on a greased cooky sheet. Bake in a 375° oven for 10 minutes, or until delicately browned. Shake the pan frequently.

Combine the honey, brown sugar, and ginger in a saucepan. Bring to a boil and cook over low heat for 10 minutes. Add the baked pastry and the nuts. Cook over low heat, stirring constantly with a wooden spoon, until thick and browned, about 5 minutes.

Wet a board with cold water. Pour the mixture onto it. Cool slightly. Shape between wet hands into 2-inch balls or squares.

> NOTE: This is an extremely rich dessert. It will keep for about 2 weeks.

Passover for me when I was a little girl was the happiest holiday of all the holidays. It meant new shoes that sang a song when I walked, a new hat and a new coat, but best of all it meant going to my grandfather and grandma's house, where all my aunts and uncles and cousins would gather together from near and far. My grandmother's table would have all the extra boards in it and would reach way out into the parlor. What happy memories. My Cousin Henry, my Aunt Jennie's youngest son, would ask my grandfather the four questions and he would explain the history of the Israelites delivered from Egypt, "and thou shalt tell thy son in that day, saying, it is because of that which the Lord did for me when I came forth out of Egypt."

All the stories of the hardships of the Israelites couldn't sadden me. I was happy. I loved the matzos, I loved the hard-boiled eggs, gefilte fish and matzo balls, and the tzimmes, *and I loved my grandparents, my relatives, and my cousins. But how long does it take to grow up? Not long enough. Now the Seder is in my house, and soon I'll be the grandma and Jake'll be the grandpa. And my table will grow bigger, too, and need all the extension boards.*

Passover, I think, will always be my happiest holiday, because no matter how old I'll be, at Passover time I'm always the little girl at my grandma's house.

CHAROSETH

A CEREMONIAL
PASSOVER PREPARATION

½ cup ground walnuts
1 apple, peeled and grated
3 tablespoons sweet wine
¼ teaspoon cinnamon
  (optional)

Mix together the walnuts, apple, wine, and cinnamon until smooth. Form into a mound. A small amount of this is eaten with matzos.

PASSOVER MEAT BLINTZES

1½ cups ground cooked meat or
  poultry
3 tablespoons grated onion
2 egg yolks
¼ teaspoon freshly ground black
  pepper
4 eggs
1 teaspoon salt
1¾ cups water
1 cup matzo cake meal
4 tablespoons shortening

Mix the meat, onion, egg yolks, and pepper until smooth. Correct seasoning. Set aside.

Beat the eggs and salt together. Add the water and mix. Add the cake meal, again mixing well.

Melt 1 teaspoon of the shortening in a 7-inch skillet. Pour 2 tablespoons of the batter into it, turning the pan quickly to cover the bottom. Fry until lightly browned on one side. Turn out onto a plate, browned side up. Stack the pancakes as they are finished, using additional shortening as required.

Place a tablespoon of the meat mixture on each pancake. Turn in the ends and roll up.

Melt the remaining shortening in a skillet and brown the *blintzes* in it.

PASSOVER RUSSELL BORSCHT (FERMENTED BEETS)

8 cups *russell* (see note p. 265)
2 cups water
3 beets, peeled and grated
2 onions, finely chopped
3 pounds beef (brisket or plate flank)
Beef bones
2 teaspoons salt
4 tablespoons sugar
2 tablespoons lemon juice
3 eggs

Combine the *russell*, water, beets, onions, beef, and beef bones in a saucepan. Bring to a boil. Skim the top. Cover and cook over medium heat for 2 hours. Add the salt, sugar, and lemon juice. Cook for 30 minutes. Correct seasoning, adding a little more sugar or lemon juice. Remove the bones and slice the meat.

Beat the eggs in a bowl. Gradually add 3 cups of the soup, beating constantly to prevent curdling.

Serve with pieces of the meat in the soup, or serve the meat as a separate course.

> NOTE: *Russell*, fermented beet juice, is prepared by the following method. About 12 very large beets should be peeled and cut into quarters. Place them in a large pot or stone jug and fill with 5 quarts of water. Use a container that will permit the 5 quarts of water to come within an inch of the top. Put the top on the container at a very slight angle and cover with a thin cloth to keep out dust. After 10 days, remove the cover and skim the surface carefully; stir well and re-cover. The *russell* should be ready for use 2 to 3 weeks later. The liquid should be completely clear, bright red, and have a winelike aroma. If preferred, *russell* may be purchased in bottles.

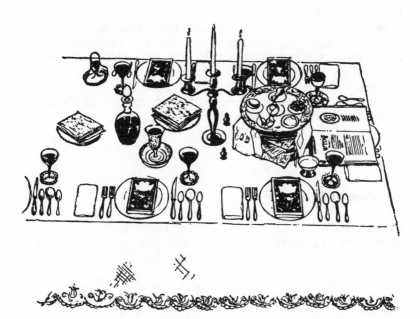

MOLLY'S PASSOVER TABLE

PASSOVER POULTRY STUFFING

½ cup boiling water
6 matzos, crumbled
4 tablespoons shortening
2 onions, chopped
3 stalks celery, chopped
Liver and gizzard of poultry,
   chopped
3 tablespoons chopped parsley
2 teaspoons salt
½ teaspoon freshly ground black
   pepper
2 eggs, beaten

Pour the boiling water over the matzos. Soak for 5 minutes. Drain.
Melt the shortening in a skillet. Add the onions and celery. Sauté
for 5 minutes, stirring frequently. Add the liver and gizzard. Sauté
for 10 minutes, stirring occasionally. Add the parsley, salt, pepper,
eggs, and matzos. Mix well. Stuff the poultry and roast in the usual
manner.

The amount specified is sufficient for a 5- to 6-pound chicken or
duck. Double the proportions for a turkey.

PASSOVER HREMSLACH

DEEP-FAT-FRIED
MATZO-MEAL PANCAKES

1 cup matzo meal
2 tablespoons ground almonds
1 teaspoon salt
1 teaspoon sugar
4 egg yolks
1 cup boiling stock or boiling
   water
4 egg whites
Fat for deep frying

Mix the matzo meal, almonds, salt, and sugar together. Add the egg yolks, mixing well. Gradually add the stock, beating constantly to prevent curdling.

Beat the egg whites until stiff but not dry. Fold them into the matzo-meal mixture carefully.

Heat the fat to 370°. Drop the mixture in by the tablespoonful. Fry until browned on both sides, about 5 minutes. Drain well. Serve with honey, jelly, or confectioners' sugar.

KNEIDLACH MIT FLAUMENT

DUMPLINGS AND PRUNES

1½ pounds unsweetened prunes, presoaked and pitted
2 cups water
¾ cup sugar
1 lemon, sliced thin
4 egg yolks
4 tablespoons melted shortening
¾ teaspoon salt
1 cup matzo meal
4 egg whites
½ cup almonds

Combine the prunes, water, sugar, and lemon slices in a saucepan. Bring to a boil and cook over low heat for 15 minutes.

Beat the egg yolks. Add the shortening, salt, and matzo meal. Mix well. Beat the egg whites until stiff but not dry and fold into the previous mixture. Between wet hands shape the mixture into 1-inch balls. Press an almond into each. Arrange the balls in a greased baking dish. Pour the prunes and juice over them.

Bake uncovered in a 350° oven for 35 minutes. Serve as an accompaniment to main-course dishes.

PASSOVER CHEESE PIE

> ½ cup shortening
> 1½ cups matzo meal
> 3 tablespoons sugar
> ½ teaspoon salt
> 1 tablespoon water

Cream the shortening. Add the matzo meal, sugar, and salt, mixing very well. Add the water gradually. Pat the mixture into a 10-inch pie plate. Now prepare the filling:

> ½ pound cream cheese
> ½ pound cottage cheese
> 3 egg yolks
> ¾ cup sugar
> 1 tablespoon potato starch
> 1 cup sour cream
> 1 teaspoon grated lemon rind
> 3 egg whites

Force the cream cheese and cottage cheese through a sieve. (This step may be omitted if an electric mixer is used for the later steps.) Beat the cheese mixture until fluffy. Add the egg yolks and sugar, beating until smooth. Add the potato starch, sour cream, and lemon rind. Mix well. Preheat oven to 350°.

Beat the egg whites until stiff but not dry. Fold them into the cheese mixture carefully but thoroughly. Pour into the prepared pie plate.

Bake for 1 hour, or until a knife comes out clean.

PASSOVER CHEESE PANCAKES

½ pound cream cheese
½ pound cottage cheese
2 eggs
1 teaspoon salt
1 teaspoon sugar
1½ cups matzo meal
½ cup shortening

Beat the cream cheese and cottage cheese together until smooth and fluffy. Add the eggs, salt, sugar, and 1 cup of the matzo meal. Mix well together. Form into pancakes and dip in the remaining matzo meal.

Heat half of the shortening in a skillet. Fry the pancakes in it until browned on both sides. Add more shortening as necessary.

Serve with sour cream and sugar if desired.

PASSOVER CRULLERS

¾ cup sugar
⅓ cup water
½ teaspoon cinnamon
4 eggs
¼ teaspoon salt
½ cup matzo meal
Fat for deep frying

Combine the sugar, water, and cinnamon in a saucepan. Cook over low heat for 10 minutes, or until syrupy.

Beat the eggs and salt together until thick. Add the matzo meal, mixing well.

Heat the fat to 370°. Drop the batter into it by the teaspoonful. Fry until browned on both sides, about 2 minutes. Drain.

Serve hot. Pour the syrup over the crullers or dunk the crullers into the syrup.

MATZO-MEAL PANCAKES

4 egg yolks
½ cup cold water
½ teaspoon salt
2 tablespoons grated onion
1⅛ cups matzo meal
4 egg whites, stiffly beaten
½ cup shortening

Beat together the egg yolks, water, salt, onion, and matzo meal. Fold in the egg whites carefully but thoroughly.

Melt half the shortening in a skillet. Drop the batter by the tablespoonful and fry until lightly browned on both sides. Add additional shortening as required.

Serve hot as an accompaniment to meat dishes, or as a separate course with applesauce. If served as a breakfast pancake, omit the onion and serve with sugar.

MATZO CHARLOTTE

4 matzos
3 egg yolks
¼ cup orange juice
2 teaspoons grated orange rind
1 teaspoon salt
¾ cup sugar
3 tablespoons melted shortening
3 egg whites, stiffly beaten

Soak the matzos in cold water for 5 minutes. Drain well. Mash as fine as possible.

Beat together the egg yolks, orange juice, orange rind, salt, sugar, and 2 tablespoons of the shortening. Add the matzos and mix very well. Fold in the egg whites thoroughly. Preheat oven to 350°.

Grease a 2-quart baking dish with the remaining shortening. Pour the mixture into it.

Bake for 30 minutes, or until browned and set. Serve hot as an accompaniment to meat dishes, or as a dessert, sprinkled with sugar and cinnamon.

Mrs. Kerrigan dropped in one day for lunch and I was having matzo brie. She thought it was a wonderful dish and when she found out that it was nothing but matzo and eggs she said it sounded wonderful for her to serve for Lent. She tried it out on Mr. Kerrigan, and he said send the recipe to Ireland so his folks would have it for the Lenten season. So she sent the recipe, but they couldn't find matzo over there and so after she sent them some matzo and they tried the recipe they loved it. So every year for Lent, Mrs. Kerrigan sends matzos to Mr. Kerrigan's family in County Sligo and every year they get a letter saying how much they enjoyed the matzo brie.

MRS. KERRIGAN'S MATZO BRIE

FRIED MATZO

4 matzos
4 eggs
1½ teaspoons salt
3 tablespoons shortening

Soak the matzos in cold water for 2 minutes. Drain and crumble.

Beat the eggs and salt together in a bowl. Add the matzos, mixing until well coated.

Heat the shortening in a large skillet. Pour the mixture into it. Fry until browned on both sides.

Serve with a little sugar sprinkled on top, or with a little jelly.

MATZO-MEAL DUMPLINGS

> 1 cup matzo meal
> 1 cup boiling water
> 3 tablespoons melted shortening
> 1 egg, beaten
> 1 teaspoon salt
> ¼ teaspoon white pepper
> 1 tablespoon chopped parsley

Place the matzo meal in a bowl. Add the water, stirring constantly until thoroughly blended. Add the shortening, egg, salt, pepper, and parsley. Mix well. Chill for 1 hour.

Roll into 1-inch balls between wet palms. Drop into boiling soup or boiling salted water. Cook over low heat for 15 minutes.

PASSOVER MUFFINS

> 3 eggs
> 1 teaspoon salt
> ¾ cup milk
> 1 cup matzo meal
> ⅓ cup cake meal
> 4 tablespoons melted shortening

Beat the eggs. Add the salt and milk. Mix well together. Add the matzo meal, cake meal, and shortening. Preheat oven to 350°.

Grease a muffin tin (12 muffins). Pour the mixture into it.

Bake for 30 minutes, or until a cake tester comes out clean.

This pie is my speciality. Not by me, but by Simon.
When My Rich Cousin was just struggling, he used to eat
with us, and his favorite dessert was this pie. He said that if

he ever got rich he would have a cook and the only thing the cook had to know was how to make this pie. So when Simon got rich he hired a cook and he had her make a lemon meringue pie. It didn't turn out so so-so, and he sent the cook to me for lessons. I showed her this recipe and she's been with Simon for fifteen years now, and would you believe it, Simon still says mine is better. It's the exact same recipe as this one. Some people are just stubborn. The Passover lemon filling is so good that I use a pastry crust the rest of the year with the same filling.

PASSOVER LEMON MERINGUE PIE

1½ cups matzo meal
⅛ teaspoon salt
⅓ cup melted shortening
3 eggs
1⅛ cups sugar
6 tablespoons butter
⅓ cup lemon juice
1 tablespoon grated lemon rind
3 egg whites

Mix the matzo meal, salt, and melted shortening together. Press into a greased 9-inch pie plate.

Bake in a 350° oven for 20 minutes. Cool.

Combine the eggs, ⅞ cup of the sugar, the butter, lemon juice, and lemon rind in the top of a double boiler. Place over hot water and cook over low heat, stirring constantly, until the mixture is thick and coats the spoon. Cool. Pour into the baked pie shell.

Beat the egg whites until stiff but not dry. Fold in the remaining ¼ cup of sugar thoroughly. Pile over the lemon filling.

Bake in a 375° oven for 10 minutes, or until delicately browned on top.

MATZO-MEAL PUDDING

2 eggs
½ cup sugar
2 cups milk
4 tablespoons melted butter
1 cup matzo meal
½ teaspoon salt
2 tablespoons brandy

Beat the eggs in a bowl. Add the sugar, beating well. Add the milk and butter, and mix. Add the matzo meal, salt, and brandy. Beat well together. Pour into a buttered 2-quart casserole or baking dish.

Bake in a 350° oven for 1 hour, or until set and browned on top. Serve in place of potatoes.

PASSOVER APPLE CHARLOTTE

4 egg yolks
¾ cup sifted sugar
2 teaspoons lemon juice
1 teaspoon grated lemon rind
6 apples, peeled and grated
½ cup matzo meal
4 egg whites
⅛ teaspoon salt
2 tablespoons shortening
½ cup ground blanched almonds

Beat the egg yolks in a bowl. Add the sugar, beating until thick and light in color. Add the lemon juice, lemon rind, apples, and matzo meal. Mix well.

Beat the egg whites and salt until stiff but not dry. Fold into the apple mixture carefully. Preheat oven to 350°.

Grease a 9-inch spring-form pan with the shortening and dust with some of the almonds. Pour the mixture into it. Sprinkle the remaining almonds on top.

Bake for 40 minutes, or until set and browned on top. Carefully run a knife around the edge and remove the sides of the spring form. Serve warm or cold.

I must be the biggest amusement for my family. I don't know, but at first every time I made this spongecake my whole family made little bets, will it fall or won't it. The first time I ever made it, it fell. That was the first time and the last time. Sammy and Rosie weren't even born yet, and to hear them talk you would think they were spectators. So now it's a tradition, will it fall or not? It will not! I learned my lesson the first time, and the secret is in the recipe, but would I tell them? Not at all. Why should I spoil their fun?

PASSOVER SPONGECAKE

12 egg yolks
2 cups sifted sugar
1¼ cups potato starch
¼ cup sifted matzo meal
¼ teaspoon salt
2 tablespoons lemon juice
12 egg whites

Beat the egg yolks. Gradually add the sugar, beating until thick and light in color. Sift the potato starch, matzo meal and salt onto the yolk mixture, but do not mix. Add the lemon juice.

275

Line an oblong, oiled pan with wax paper, aluminum foil, or brown paper. Preheat oven to 325°.

Beat the egg whites until stiff, but not dry. Pile on previous mixture and fold in carefully but thoroughly. Pour into the prepared pan.

Bake for 1 hour, or until a cake tester comes out clean.

PASSOVER ALMOND MACAROONS

> 3 egg whites
> ⅛ teaspoon salt
> 1⅛ cups sugar
> 2¼ cups ground blanched
>   almonds
> 2 teaspoons matzo meal

Beat the egg whites and salt until stiff but not dry. Add the sugar, almonds, and matzo meal. Fold in thoroughly. Preheat oven to 300°.

Grease a cooky sheet and dust lightly with matzo meal. Drop the mixture by the teaspoonful, leaving space between each. If desired, half a blanched almond may be placed on each macaroon.

Bake for 15 minutes. Cool.

PASSOVER NUT COOKIES

> 3 eggs
> ½ cup sugar
> 2 tablespoons brandy
> 2¼ cups finely ground nuts
>   (hazelnuts or almonds)
> 1 tablespoon matzo meal
> ½ cup hazelnuts or almonds,
>   halved

Beat the eggs until light. Add the sugar, beating until thick. Add the brandy. Mix well. Preheat oven to 300°. Fold in the ground nuts thoroughly. Shape into 1-inch balls and place on a cooky sheet 2 inches apart in each direction. Place half of a nut in the center of each and press down gently.

Bake for 20 minutes, or until lightly browned. Loosen the cookies from the pan immediately after removing from the oven.

PASSOVER JELLY ROLL

5 egg yolks
½ cup sugar
4 tablespoons sifted potato starch
5 egg whites
6 tablespoons jelly

Grease a jelly-roll pan, about 11 x 17 inches, and line it with wax paper. Grease again.

Beat the egg yolks. Add 5 tablespoons of the sugar, beating until thick and light in color. Add the potato starch. Mix well. Preheat oven to 400°.

Beat the egg whites until stiff but not dry. Fold into the egg-yolk mixture thoroughly. Pour into the pan.

Bake for 12 minutes, or until a cake tester comes out clean.

Sprinkle the remaining sugar on a large piece of wax paper. Turn the cake out onto it. Remove the paper in which it was baked. Roll up the cake carefully and cool. Unroll, spread with the jelly, and roll up tightly. Chill.

PASSOVER PARTY CAKE

¾ cup sifted sugar
1 cup finely ground blanched
   almonds
6 egg whites
2 tablespoons potato starch

Mix the sugar and almonds together. Beat the egg whites until stiff but not dry. Fold in the nut mixture gently. Preheat oven to 300°.

Grease two 9-inch layer-cake pans and dust lightly with the potato starch. Pour the mixture into them evenly, smoothing the tops. Bake 40 minutes.

Cool. Spread whipped cream between the layers and over the top, or ice with the following filling:

½ cup sugar
⅓ cup freshly brewed coffee
4 egg yolks
¼ pound sweet butter
½ cup heavy cream, whipped

Boil the sugar and coffee for 10 minutes. Beat the egg yolks in the top of a double boiler. Gradually add the coffee syrup, stirring constantly. Place over hot water and cook, stirring constantly until mixture coats the spoon. Strain and cool.

Cream the butter, gradually adding the egg yolk mixture. Mix well. Fold in the whipped cream.

Spread between the layers and on the top of the cake.

And

MENUS

COOKING TERMS

COOKING HINTS

TEMPERATURE GUIDE

EQUIVALENT WEIGHTS AND MEASURES

MENUS

FRIDAY NIGHT DINNER

Cold Boiled Fish or Gefilte Fish with Horseradish
Chicken Soup with Kreplach
Chicken and Rice
Carrot Tzimmes   Cabbage Strudel
Fruit and Nut Compote
Komishbrot   Tea or Black Coffee

SATURDAY DINNER

Chopped Liver
Dried Mushroom Soup
Baked Veal Chops   Chulent
Honey Cookies   Tea or Black Coffee

Menus

COMPANY DINNER

Jellied Carp with Grapes
Vegetable Soup
Veal Paprikas, Onion Dumplings
Sweet and Sour String Beans   Rice Kugel
Nut Spongecake   Tea or Black Coffee

HOLIDAY DINNER

Pickled Fish or Gefilte Fish
Beef Soup with Farfel
Roast Duck
Potato Charlotte   Sweet and Sour Red Cabbage
Fruit Strudel   Tea or Black Coffee

DAIRY DINNER

Vegetable Chicken Livers
Mushroom Soup
Fish in Sour Cream
Rice Stuffed Peppers
Cheese Pudding   Coffee

ONE-DISH DINNER

Hot Meat Borscht   Kashe Varnishkes
Prune Tzimmes   Tea or Black Coffee

PASSOVER SEDER DINNER

Ceremonial Foods
Gefilte Fish with Beet Horseradish
Chicken Soup with Matzo-Meal Dumplings
Stuffed Turkey   Carrot Sticks in Honey
Passover Jelly Roll   Tea

PASSOVER DINNER

Russell Borscht with Boiled Potatoes
Matzo-Meal Pudding
Nut Cookies and Tea

PASSOVER DAIRY DINNER

Paprika Fish
Passover Cheese Pancakes
Lemon Pie   Coffee

PASSOVER LUNCH

Chopped Eggs and Onions
Matzo Brie   Coffee

COMMON COOKING TERMS

BAKE   To cook by means of dry heat, usually in an oven

BASTE   To spoon liquid over a food while marinating or cooking

BATTER   Any combination of flour, eggs, milk, or water used as dipping, coating, or for pancakes or cake

BEAT   To mix, using a wire whisk, fork, rotary or electric beater

BLANCH   To place in cold water, then bring to a boil. Nuts are blanched in this manner, then the skins are slipped off between the fingers

BLEND   To mix ingredients together until smooth

BOIL   To heat a mixture or liquid until bubbles appear on the surface; also to continue the process

BOILING POINT   The temperature at which a liquid begins to bubble around the edge

BRAISE   To brown in a little fat, then cook over low heat with very little liquid in a covered pan

283

BROIL   To cook by direct heat close to the source of the heat

BRUSH   To spread seasoning, butter, or other coating

CHILL   To cool by placing under refrigeration

CHOP   To cut into small pieces

COMBINE   To join two or more ingredients together

CREAM   To soften ingredients by beating with a spoon, rotary or electric beater until soft and of creamy consistency

CUBE   To cut into pieces with approximately six equal sides

CUT IN SHORTENING   To mix shortening with flour by using a pastry blender or two knives until shortening is evenly distributed

DISSOLVE   To melt, break up, or liquefy

DREDGE   To coat well, usually with flour or sugar

DRIPPINGS   Fat or juices that cook out of foods

DUST   To sprinkle lightly with a dry coating such as bread crumbs, flour, or sugar

FLAKE   To separate foods with a fork

FOLD IN   To use a spoon in a gently rolling circular movement as a means of combining ingredients

FRY   To cook in hot oil or other fat

GARNISH   To decorate

GRATE   To rub into small pieces on a grater

GRIND   To put through a food mill or chopper; to reduce or crush into small pieces

KNEAD To manipulate or work with the hands, usually a dough, using a folding-back and pressing-forward motion

MARINADE A liquid used for pickling or seasoning by soaking; usually contains vinegar or wine, oil, spices, and herbs

MARINATE To soak in a marinade

MELT To heat until the ingredient is changed from solid to liquid

MINCE To chop as fine as possible

MIX To stir ingredients together

PAN-BROIL To cook in a hot skillet with little or no fat

PAN-FRY To cook in a frying pan over direct heat, using some oil or fat

PARBOIL To cook partially in water or other liquids

PARE To remove the outside skin or peel of vegetables, fruits, etc.

POACH To cook over a liquid just below the boiling point

PREHEAT To turn on the oven to a selected temperature about 10 minutes before it is to be used

PURÉE Food, usually cooked, forced through a sieve or run in an electric blender to produce a smooth mixture; to force through a sieve

RENDER To melt solid fat away from connective tissue; to clarify fats by melting

ROAST To cook in an oven

ROLL To place on a flat surface and spread thin with a rolling pin

SAUTÉ To cook or brown over low heat in a little fat, oil, or butter

SCALD To pour boiling water over a food; to heat almost to boiling

SEAR To brown a food at high heat

SIEVE A utensil with a perforated bottom, used to separate coarse pieces from fine, and as a strainer of liquids

SIFT To separate coarse pieces from fine by shaking through a sieve, thus removing lumps and foreign particles

SIMMER To cook over low heat just below the boiling point

SKEWER To fasten with a wood or metal pin to hold something in place while cooking; a wood or metal pin

SOAK To cover a food with liquid

SPATULA Broad flexible knife suitable for lifting foods

STALK An individual piece; in celery the various stalks make up a bunch

STEAM To cook by direct contact with live steam in a covered container

STEEP To soak in hot liquid below the boiling point

STIR To mix ingredients together, usually with a spoon

STOCK Broth in which meat, poultry, bones, or fish have been cooked

WHIP To beat a liquid to a froth; to increase the volume of a liquid by beating air into it

COOKING HINTS

BAKING Always have ingredients at room temperature.

DAIRY PRODUCTS Use sweet butter whenever possible.

DRIED FRUITS To chop dried fruits more easily, heat the knife or food chopper before using.

FISH Remove fish from the refrigerator 30 minutes before using.

MEATS Remove from refrigerator 1 hour before using.

NUTS To blanch nuts, cover with cold water, bring to a boil, drain, cover with cold water, and slip the skin off between the fingers.

POTATOES Grate potatoes into salted water to keep from turning dark.

POULTRY Season the day before it is to be used whenever possible. Remove from refrigerator 1 hour before cooking.

287

SOUR MILK AND CREAM If not available, add 2 teaspoons of lemon juice or vinegar to each cup of liquid; cook until the boiling point; cool and use.

YEAST Yeast is sold compressed (fresh) or dry in 1-ounce packages. Always scald milk, then cool to lukewarm before adding yeast.

TEMPERATURE GUIDE

Very slow oven	225°
Slow oven	250° to 300°
Moderate oven	325° to 375°
Hot oven	400° to 450°
Very hot oven	450° and over

NOTE: Always preheat oven 10 minutes before it is to be used.

COOKING MEASUREMENTS

Dash	Less than ⅛ teaspoon
3 teaspoons	1 tablespoon
2 liquid tablespoons	1 ounce
4 tablespoons	¼ cup
16 tablespoons	1 cup
1 cup	½ pint
2 liquid cups	1 pound
16 ounces	1 pound
4 cups	1 quart

EQUIVALENT WEIGHTS AND MEASURES

BAKING POWDER	1 ounce	3½ tablespoons
BEANS, DRIED	½ pound	1 cup
BREAD CRUMBS	3 oz. (approx.)	1 cup
BUTTER AND SOLID FATS	1 pound	2 cups
BUTTER AND SOLID FATS	¼ pound	8 tablespoons
BUTTER AND SOLID FATS	¼ pound	½ cup
CHEESE, COTTAGE	½ pound	1 cup
CHEESE, CREAM	½ pound	1 cup
CHEESE. GRATED	¼ pound	1 cup
CHOCOLATE, UNSWEETENED	1 ounce	1 square
CINNAMON	1 ounce	4½ tablespoons
COCONUT, DRIED GRATED	¼ pound	1 cup, packed
CONSOMMÉ	1 can	10½ ounces

CORN MEAL	1 pound	3 cups
CORNSTARCH	4½ ounces	1 cup
CRACKER CRUMBS	5 ounces	1 cup
CREAM	½ pint	1 cup
CREAM, WHIPPED	1 cup unwhipped	2 cups whipped
DATES, PITTED	½ pound	1¼ cups
EGGS	2 ounces	1 egg
EGGS	5	1 cup
EGG WHITES	8–10	1 cup
FLOUR	1 pound	4 cups, sifted
FLOUR	¼ ounce	1 tablespoon
HONEY	12 ounces	1 cup
LEMON JUICE	1 lemon	2–3 tablespoons
LEMON RIND	1 lemon	2–3 teaspoons
MACARONI, UNCOOKED	4 ounces	1 cup
NUTS, GROUND	¼ pound	1 cup
OIL	7½ ounces	1 cup
PEANUT BUTTER	1 pound	1¾ cups
POTATOES	1 pound	3 average
PRUNES	1 pound	2½ cups
RAISINS	1 pound	3 cups

Equivalent Weights and Measures

RICE, UNCOOKED	1 pound	2 cups
RICE, UNCOOKED	1 cup	3 cups, cooked
SUGAR, BROWN	1 pound	2¼ cups, packed
SUGAR, CONFECTIONERS'	1 pound	3½–4 cups, sifted
SUGAR, GRANULATED	1 pound	2 cups
TOMATOES, FRESH	1 pound	3 average
TOMATO SAUCE (1 CAN)	7¾–8 ounces	1 cup
WINE	1 wineglass	4–5 tablespoons

History of Kosher Food

and

The Story of Passover

There is nothing better for a man,
than that he should eat and drink,
and that he should make his soul
enjoy good in his labour.

ECCLESIASTES 2:24

KOSHER FOOD AND HOW IT BEGAN

To begin with, there have been regulations for the preparation of food for almost three thousand years. But no explanation can be understood unless there is a little knowledge of the background of the Jewish people.

The very earliest history of the Jews is in considerable doubt because written records are not available, but there was undoubtedly a tribe with Semitic origins living in the Chaldean region. Later they lived in the area known as Goshen, in the northeastern part of what was then Egypt, about 1350 B.C. Subsequently the people were taken into slavery by the Egyptians, where they received cruel treatment. Moses led his people from bondage about the year 1220 B.C. They wandered about in the desert and then finally arrived in what we now know as the Holy Land. There began a period of greatness for the Jewish people. Tribes were united under leaders called Judges, a word that has survived to the present day. King David brought peace and wealth to his nation. His son was Solomon, famed in song and story, and the man who built the great Temple at Jerusalem.

But great as Solomon was, his methods of taxation caused many protests, and after his death there followed a time of confusion and disruption. The country broke into two parts (much like our own war between the states, when the North was pitted against the South).

The north formed a kingdom known as Israel, and the south was called Judah. The two halves battled fiercely, although intermittently, for two centuries beginning about 935 B.C. Then Saigon II captured the north, thus leading to the exile of the Israelites and the legend of the ten lost tribes of Israel. While it is true that a large number of people vanished without leaving a trace, what actually happened to them is more a matter of conjecture than of fact. Scholars of the future may or may not solve the mystery; at present no proof is available. There are those who believe that the ten tribes emigrated toward India and the East; others believe that they turned toward Africa and became the so-called "black Jews" or Ethiopian Jews, of whom there are actually a considerable number. In various cities throughout the United States, but particularly in New York, there are various congregations of colored Jews practicing orthodox Judaism. Another theory is the Anglo-Israelite view, which firmly believes that England was partly settled by these lost tribes. In any event, during the seventeenth century this theory permitted many Jews to re-enter England.

The southern part, Judah, was conquered by the Assyrians, Egyptians, and Babylonians. The great Temple at Jerusalem was destroyed and the people exiled. Later they returned to Jerusalem with the approval of Cyrus the Great, leader of the Persian Empire, who is thought to have wanted another country between himself and powerful Egypt, much as modern nations arrange "buffer states" between themselves and another important power. Although the returned Jews were dominated by the Greeks, they finally won their freedom again under the leadership of Judas Maccabeus, who in 165 B.C. led them on to victory. But it was all in vain, for shortly thereafter the

Roman legions took control of Jerusalem and the surrounding country; the city was finally destroyed about A.D. 70.

Now there was nothing to be gained by remaining, and the people
dispersed in all directions of the compass. Wagons and caravans
moved to the north, east, south, and west, although chiefly they went
to Europe. Spain in particular became a center of Jewish life and
culture. The centuries went by, the Middle Ages, when life moved
slowly. The homeland was not forgotten, only laid away temporarily
in the minds of the exiled Jews. As if to compensate, they practiced
their religion all the more fiercely and clung to it, for it was all they
had left in the world.

The Crusades came, and with them a series of laws expelling the
Jews from their adopted countries. In 1290 they were forced to leave
England; in 1392, France; in 1492, Spain, and in 1497 they left
Portugal. Those who were lucky enough to escape went anyplace
they could, but many fled to Turkey and Holland, where they were
welcomed. A large group settled in Russia, Poland, Austria, Rumania,
and Germany, as well as in many of the other neighboring countries.

With this historical background, it is now possible to understand
the development of Jewish laws and practices regarding food. According to Jewish history, the very earliest laws concerning food and
diet were given to the people by Moses just prior to leaving Egypt.
This is discussed in more detail in the section on Passover. It is extremely difficult at the present time, some thirty centuries later, to
say whether or not Moses or some other person or group actually
gave the laws to the people, and there is a certain amount of difference of opinion on this subject by Biblical scholars. After Moses,
there are the five books of the Bible, the Pentateuch, and in particular the section called Leviticus, which sets forth rules regarding which
foods may or may not be consumed.

But the rules of Moses and the books of the Bible were only a
beginning. They were followed by that pillar of Judaism, the *Talmud*,
the learning. These books are in effect a compendium of the oral laws

of the Jews, as opposed to the written laws, the Scriptures. The *Talmud* itself subdivides into two principal parts: the *Mishna*, which was written in Hebrew, and the *Gemara*, prepared in Aramaic, an old Semitic language. Many people carelessly refer to the *Gemara* as the *Talmud*, but this is not quite a correct usage, since the *Gemara* is only half of the *Talmud*. Much of the *Mishna* was codified by King Judah I, although part of the basic work was prepared by two important scholars, Hillel and Shammai. It is thought that the so-called Babylonian *Talmud* was completed about the year A.D. 500.

The *Mishna* is indeed a detailed book, filled with rules and regulations on almost every conceivable phase in the life of the people, but it was not sufficiently meticulous for those scholars of the period whose principal delight in life was raising abstruse and exotic arguments over hypothetical and technical situations. To settle many of the points which were intended to be disposed of in the *Mishna*, a series of commentaries came into existence known as the *Gemara*. This is a compilation of lore and knowledge intended to explain the *Mishna* and the problems it raised in its own explanations. The *Mishna* itself consists of six principal orders, called *sedarim*, and sixty-three separate units. Only thirty-six and one half of these units have a commentary in the *Gemara*. The *Gemara* may be compared only to a scholarly maze, for once in it, it is unlikely that you will find your way out of it during your lifetime. Certainly those scholars of the Middle Ages gloried in a lifetime of study, spending delightful months and years arguing and discussing problems which would not likely arise. It is a compilation of miscellaneous information on almost every conceivable subject, including food, law, medicine, astronomy, and hundreds of other subjects. The *Gemara* itself may be divided into the legal discussions, or *halakah*, and the *hagadah*, which is filled with folklore and fables. In addition to the *Gemara*, there is a world of literature by Jewish scholars in every land, and these are, in effect, commentaries on the *Gemara*.

Then, to round off the entire picture, there is the *Shulchan*

Aruch, the prepared table, most of which was written about A.D. 1520 to 1600. This sets forth in codified form the rules and regulations regarding food and its preparation.

Many of the earliest instructions regarding food go back to the books of the Bible, notably Exodus, Leviticus, and Deuteronomy. These books state: "Thou shall not seethe a kid in its mother's milk." Seethe, in Biblical usage, means to cook. In practice, this was understood to mean that meat of any sort could not be cooked together with milk. As time went by, the prohibition was extended to milk derivatives such as cheese. Subsequently the rule was even further extended as a prohibition against having meat dishes and milk dishes in the same meal, except that a separate meat dish may be served after a dairy dish. Once meat is eaten, no dairy products may be consumed until at least six hours have elapsed.

With a few exceptions, Jewish people recognize four principal food divisions (Passover food is discussed separately):

1. *Milchig*, OR DAIRY FOODS. These include sweet butter, milk, sweet and sour cream, buttermilk, and cheese. Orthodox Jews do not use canned milk or salt butter.

2. *Fleischig*, OR MEATS. Included in this group are all meats and poultry (except those classified as *trefe*), including all of the various variety meats, such as liver, sweetbreads, etc. All *fleischig* foods must be killed according to the ritual law on the subject, the *shechitah*. The ritual law will be discussed later in this chapter.

3. *Pareve*, OR NEUTRAL FOODS. These are neither meats nor dairy food, and as such may be mixed with meat or dairy dishes. They include such foods as vegetables, fruits, fish, and eggs. Certain fish are *trefe*, and these are of course not *pareve*. Eggs are free of restrictions except that they must not have any spot of blood in them, since blood is a prohibited food and thus *trefe*. Should an egg be found in poultry, it is forbidden to cook the egg with dairy foods.

4. *Trefe* (also called *trefah*), OR PROHIBITED FOODS. Jewish people do not eat pork, shellfish, or blood of any animal or fowl. Leviticus II is the authority which says: "Whatsoever parteth the hoof, and is clovenfooted, and cheweth the cud, among the beasts, that shall ye eat." Later interpretations have amplified this first instruction so that it is now generally understood to mean that the only animals fit for consumption are those without upper teeth, but having a split hoof, which chew their cud and have four legs (thus eliminating the monkey and kangaroo, for example). The pig, of course, does not chew the cud, although it does have a cloven hoof. Mohammedans, too, do not eat pork, and in India there are religious sects which avoid pork in any form, thus supporting the theory of those who believe that the lost tribes mentioned above may have settled in India.

It is not possible today to prove that the ancient scholars knew that pork carries the virulent trichinosis, since nowhere in the books is there any mention of the disease-carrying potential of pigs. On the other hand, it may be argued that the law-givers knew this fact and worded the law in such a fashion as to eliminate pork from the diet. Even today, with modern inspection, refrigeration, and advanced rules for the preparation of food, trichinosis is not an unknown disease in the United States. Elsewhere in the world it is quite common. In the sub-tropical climate of the Near East where these people lived, it is not difficult to visualize the unsanitary conditions of some three thousand years ago when these laws were first promulgated.

The requirements for birds are that they may not be birds of prey or scavengers. This eliminates hawks, vultures, and the like. Also, they must have a hind toe; although actually the Bible refers to a front toe, it has been interpreted to refer to a hind toe. The most commonly used poultry are duck, chicken, and domesticated turkey and goose. The use of wild geese and turkeys is still in some doubt.

Leviticus again is the authority regarding the consumption of fish.

"These shall ye eat of all that are in the water: whatsoever hath fins and scales." No shellfish may be eaten, since these do not have fins and scales. The theory behind this is undoubtedly the fact that shell-fish do not move about freely in the water, but tend to remain in one place. If that place is contaminated, the shellfish will be contaminated, whereas fish with fins and scales move readily in the water, seldom remaining in one place for any length of time. Therefore, according to Biblical edict, shrimp, lobsters, crabs, turtles, clams, and eels are not to be eaten. It should be remembered that these prohibitions were laid down about thirty centuries ago in a country having an extremely hot climate and during a time when people had only the most primitive ideas regarding health and sanitation. Waste matter was dumped into nearby waters as a matter of course. The law-givers of that day knew that not every shellfish was contaminated or likely to become so, but the danger was there, and for the sake of simplicity formulated a rule that could be understood by the simplest of their people.

There can be no doubt that the rules and regulations were advanced with one primary purpose in mind—the health of the people. Although many of the food injunctions have become interwoven with religious procedures, and although over the centuries observance of kosher food restrictions have become a part of the life of a religious Jew, the original purpose was to protect the people. Today, dozens of centuries later, many of the injunctions seem unnecessary to present-day descendants of those early Jews, and they are often disregarded by them. On the other hand, there are hundreds of thousands of people who still follow kosher practice precisely as it was formulated thousands of years ago.

But all of the above merely discusses which foods are fit and not fit to eat, and which combinations are permitted. Under no circumstances may *trefe* foods be eaten, and even some permitted foods require special attention. *Milchig* (dairy) foods and *pareve* (neutral) foods require no further attention, but meat and poultry (*fleischig*) may be slaughtered only according to the complex laws of *shechitah*, the ritualistic laws. Only a qualified person, called a *schochet*, is permitted to slaughter cattle or poultry, since the intent of the law was to cause the animal as little pain as possible and to permit the maximum effusion of blood. Even more blood must be removed by the *kashering* process, which the housewife does in her own home. Only the forequarters of cattle may ordinarily be consumed, since the hindquarters (although actually more desirable as food) contain too many veins filled with blood to comply. To make hindquarters fit for use, the veins must be removed with great care by hand; otherwise it is not fit, not kosher. At the time of slaughtering, the *schochet* (who is specially trained for this purpose) examines the animal carefully for signs of disease or internal lesions; all those that do not qualify must be rejected. This is an involved examination involving the lungs, liver, spleen, and other parts of the animal. At the present time many of these early regulations have become adopted into our present-day laws regarding the inspection of slaughtered cattle.

Blood of any animal or fowl is *trefe*, forbidden. The rules prohibiting the eating of pork or shellfish are easily understood on a health basis and have been previously discussed. But why this prohibition against blood? Leviticus states that blood is the life of the flesh, and while this is only symbolically correct, there is considerable truth in the statement. It is possible that the early law-givers felt that, by removing the lifeblood from the animal, the people were not eating a being that had once lived and walked on the face of the earth. Another theory which is well supported is that man is naturally a creature of violence; the scholars were trying to wean him away from a life of lawlessness into a life of living by the book and the law. Primitive peoples always thought (and still do) that eating certain parts of animals endowed them with the strength of the animal which they had consumed. A few African tribes believe that eating the heart of a tiger will give them the courage of that tiger, and possibly it was to prevent the development of warlike natures that blood was forbidden. Certainly this prohibition does not fit as readily into classification as a health safeguard as the other restrictions so easily do.

After meat has been ritualistically slaughtered, the housewife must continue with the process of removing as much blood as possible. The meat must be submerged in cold water for half an hour. It is rinsed and sprinkled with a handful of coarse salt and then placed on a grooved or perforated board for one hour, tilted so that additional blood will drain from the meat. Since broiling removes blood from meat, the requirements for *kashering* meat in the home are not necessary if the food is prepared in this fashion.

Meats which have been properly slaughtered according to *kashruth* are entitled to certificates to this effect called *heksherim,* and these are often placed on meats or canned goods. In passing, it may be said that kosher butchers charge about 25 per cent more per pound for meat than do ordinary butcher shops, owing in part to the additional expenses involved.

It has been mentioned above that dairy and meat dishes may not ordinarily be eaten at the same meal. In practice, this means that the orthodox Jewish housewife must have two sets of dishes, one for meat and one for dairy. These may not be intermingled and must be kept in separate cabinets. In addition, there must be two sets of cooking utensils, and every single pot or pan must be used either for meat or dairy, not both. Naturally there must be two sets of silverware to accompany the dishes. In the Passover section you will learn there are two additional sets of both dishes and silverware required for that period, so that the orthodox home must have a minimum of four sets of tableware. The same number of different towels are necessary. The soap must be made of vegetable fat, as most other soaps are made of non-kosher meat fats.

No work of any sort may be performed on the Sabbath, which commences with sundown of Friday and ends twenty-four hours later. No cooking can take place on Friday night or Saturday. However, previously prepared food may be warmed, provided it is done on a fire which was lit before the Sabbath began.

In the Introduction, mention has been made of the reason why no type of shortening has been specified in the recipes. Keeping the explanation of the *kashruth* in mind, the recipes in this book can be used in the kosher manner by following the rules set forth therein.

THE STORY OF PASSOVER

In the section on kosher food, a little of the varied and colorful history of the Jewish people is briefly described. You will recall that the early Jews were enslaved about the year 1300 B.C. by the Egyptians. The Bible recites the hardships of these enslaved people, forced to work long hours in the hot sun for their cruel masters. Endlessly they built and constructed cities for the Pharaohs.

The Egyptians feared the Jews in their midst, for they were numerous, and ordered that all sons born to Jews should be cast into the river, although daughters would be permitted to live. Moses, as an infant, was left in the bulrushes in the hope of avoiding his death but was reputedly rescued and reared by Pharaoh's daughter. When Moses had grown to maturity, God appeared and instructed Moses to tell Pharaoh to let his people go. Pharaoh not only refused, but ordered his taskmasters to give the slaves even more work than before. After another refusal by Pharaoh, the Lord turned the river into blood, and there was no water for the Egyptians to drink. But this was of no avail, for Pharaoh hardened his heart and would not let them go. Then the Lord commanded Moses to tell Pharaoh that if his people were still held there would be a plague of frogs, and so it came to pass that a plague of frogs covered Egypt, filling the land and the houses. Pharaoh called upon Moses to have the plague removed and promised that the Jews could go into the desert as they wished and offer prayers to their God if only the plague of frogs were removed. The plague was lifted, but thereupon Pharaoh withdrew his pledge. Then came swarms of flies, and the entire country was filled with flies, and again Pharaoh promised Moses that he would let his people go. But when the swarms left, Pharaoh again failed to live up to his word. Whereupon the Lord told Moses that he would cause the death of all the cattle; and so it was, and Pharaoh again made a promise and did not abide by his promise. Then came thunder and fire the like of which Egypt had never known. Then came a plague of locusts which covered the ground and ate up every leaf and green thing; then followed a period of darkness which lasted for three full days.

But even patience has its limit, and Moses told Pharaoh, "Thus saith the Lord, About midnight will I go out into the midst of Egypt: And all the firstborn in the land of Egypt shall die, from the firstborn of Pharaoh that sitteth upon his throne, even unto the firstborn of the maidservant that is behind the mill; and all the firstborn of beasts. And there shall be a great cry throughout all the land of Egypt, such as there was none like it, nor shall be like it any more. But against any of the children of Israel shall not a dog move his tongue, against man or beast: that ye may know how that the Lord doth put a difference between the Egyptians and Israel."

But Moses told the children of Israel: "Draw out and take you a lamb according to your families, and kill the passover. . . . For the Lord will pass through to smite the Egyptians; and when he seeth the blood upon the lintel, and on the two side posts, the Lord will pass over the door, and will not suffer the destroyer to come in unto your houses to smite you. And ye shall observe this thing for an ordinance to thee and to thy sons for ever. And it shall come to pass, when ye come to the land which the Lord will give you, according as he hath promised, that ye shall keep this service. And it shall come to pass, when your children shall say unto you, What mean ye by this service? That ye shall say, It is the sacrifice of the Lord's passover, who passed over the houses of the children of Israel in Egypt, when he smote the Egyptians, and delivered our houses."

And so it came to pass that the firstborn of the Egyptians died, and then finally did Pharaoh realize the power of the Lord and told Moses that his people could go. They gathered up their possessions, and their bread that had not risen, the unleavened bread, and set out into the desert.

But Moses told the people, "Remember this day, in which ye came out from Egypt, out of the house of bondage; for by strength of hand the Lord brought you out from this place: there shall no leavened bread be eaten. . . . Seven days thou shalt eat unleavened bread, and in the seventh day shall be a feast unto the Lord. Unleavened bread shall be eaten seven days; and there shall no leavened bread be seen with thee, neither shall there be leaven seen with thee in all thy quarters. And thou shalt shew thy son in that day, saying, This is done because of that which the Lord did unto me when I came forth out of Egypt. . . . Thou shalt therefore keep this ordinance in his season from year to year."

To this very day, Jews all over the world remember their flight to freedom under Moses, the *Pesach*, a happy holiday filled with cheer and homecoming.

The days preceding Passover are busy ones for the housewife. Since only unleavened bread is permitted, all bread, flour products, and other *chometz* (anything not permitted during Passover) must be removed. The special dishes, flatware, and kitchen utensils required for the holiday will take their place. It is also customary to clean the house and often to redecorate.

When the day of Passover comes, the table is set with the finest that the house can furnish. Gleaming candlesticks usually occupy the center of the table, and it is customary for the mother of the family to give the benediction over the ceremony of lighting the candles. Of course the unleavened bread which Moses told his people to eat, the matzos, are placed upon the table. Although three thousand years have passed since this injunction was issued, there has never been a time when Jews all over the world have failed to eat matzos during the Passover week in remembrance of their forebears who fled from Egypt. Also on the table are several other symbolic objects: *beitzah*, a roasted egg, symbolizes the loss of the Great Temple at Jerusalem where it was customary to bring offerings; *charoset*, a chopped mixture of nuts, apples, and wine, symbolizes the clay and mortar used in constructing buildings while enslaved by the Egyptians; *moror*, or bitter herbs, is to remind everyone of the bitterness of slavery (this usually consists of small pieces of fresh horseradish); *zroah*, a roasted lamb bone, signifies the old custom of roasting the Paschal lamb; *karpas*, sweet herbs, is indicative of springtime and hope (this is usually a piece of lettuce or parsley); salt water in individual bowls is to recall that the people of Israel shed many tears during their period of enslavement. A glass of wine is placed at each person's setting, and it is customary to drink four glasses of wine during the evening's services; this symbolizes the four promises made by the Lord to redeem them from the slavery of the Egyptians. In addition, an extra glass is filled with wine expressly against the coming of the prophet Elijah, who is believed to be the messenger of God to tell of the coming of the Messiah. During the services, the door to the home is opened symbolically to permit the entrance of Elijah.

The services themselves are often quite enchanting with their mixture of history, legends, old stories, and songs. At each place is a *hagadah*, a *Seder* book, which contains the Passover service. The first portion of the service concerns itself with the history of the Jews in bondage to the Egyptians and mentions the various symbols of enslavement described previously. The youngest person present asks the *mah nishtanah,* the four questions. These begin with "Why is this night different from all other nights? On all other nights we eat leavened or unleavened bread, but on this night only unleavened bread." After the Passover meal is eaten, there are prayers of thanks to the Lord for deliverance from bondage. Later there are many traditional songs, such as *"Dayainu"* (It Would Have Sufficed Us), and *"Chad Ga Ya"* (An Only Kid).

INDEX

All recipes serve 6

Index